Authenticity

Journal With

Ola Olaleye

50 Days Devotional to embrace your true self

AUTHENTICITY JOURNAL WITH OLA OLALEYE
50 Days Devotional to embrace your true self

ISBN: 978-1-7395383-8-5

Published by:
Grace House Publishing Company
www.gracehousepublishing.org

Unless otherwise indicated, all Scripture quotations are taken from the New International Version (NIV) of the Bible.

Dedication

This devotional is dedicated to my three wonderful children, Durotimi, Kiisha and Ariara

Introduction

What comes to your mind whenever you hear the word 'Authenticity'?

I bet you thought about 'Original', 'Unique', 'Genuine', or 'Real'.

According to the Cambridge Dictionary, Authenticity is the quality of being real or true.

These are all correct definitions.

Now, how would you picture your authentic self?

Perfect, Well-mannered, Religious, Clean, Blameless...

The words above are what almost 90% of human beings will use to describe their authentic self because that's how they want to imagine themselves. However, God's idea of authenticity is people who have set themselves apart to live for God by all means, and even when life gets hard, and they make mistakes or get frustrated, they will run back to God.

Authenticity in Christ is Living a "Christ-like" life.

Authentic people acknowledge God in all their doings; they don't think too highly of themselves, nor are they timid. They have confidence in Christ.

God knows that this journey of life won't be easy because of the flesh we carry, but he is always there to see us through if we hold his hands firmly.

That's why this journal is written to remind you of how God sees you and how you can live an authentic life in Christ.

Let's take a walk towards living a life of authenticity...

It's difficult because you are doing it with your common mind and neglecting God's help and guidance.

1

EMBRACING GOD'S AUTHENTIC LOVE

Scripture:

> *"For God so loved the world that he gave his one and only Son, that whoever believes in him shall not perish but have eternal life"* **John 3:16** (NIV).

Devotional

God thought so highly of us that he sent his only begotten son to die for us after making us in his own likeness. That's love, an unconditional love that can't be comprehended by the human mind.

Amidst the societal pressure to conform, fit into moulds, and project an image of perfection, the concept of authenticity can sometimes seem distant and difficult to attain. However, in the light of John 3:16, we find the remarkable truth that God sees us as authentic in His eyes, which is the perspective that matters most.

1. God's Love for the Authentic You:

"*For God so loved the world...*" These words remind us that God's love is all-encompassing. He loves you for who you are and with all your strengths and weaknesses. There is no need to put on a mask or pretend to be someone you're not. God's love extends to the authentic you. He knows your heart and loves you for your uniqueness.

2. God's Sacrifice for the Authentic You:

"*...that he gave his one and only Son...*" God's love isn't based on your performance or appearance. He loved you so much that He gave His Son, Jesus, as a sacrifice to save you from sin and offer you eternal life. This act of love reveals that God values your authenticity, not the perfect image you might present to the world.

3. God's Promise to the Authentic You:

"*...that whoever believes in him shall not perish but have eternal life.*" God's promise is for those who believe in His Son, not for those who have it all together. His promise is for the authentic, imperfect, and honest hearts who recognise their need for Him, believing that He alone can save and deliver them. God sees your authenticity, and His promise is eternal life for those who trust in Him genuinely.

God's view of authenticity is far different from the world's shallow standards. He sees your heart, your struggles, and your genuine self and loves you with an authentic and unchanging love. In God's eyes, you are enough just as you are. There is no need to wear a mask or strive for perfection to earn His love.

Today, as you meditate on John 3:16, remember that God's love is deeply authentic. Embrace your true self, warts and all, knowing that God loves and accepts you just as you are. His authentic love is an invitation to be real with Him, find comfort and belonging in His presence, and live in the liberating joy of being loved for who you truly are.

Prayer:

Heavenly Father,

Thank you for your authentic love that sees me as I am and loves me without conditions. Help me embrace my authenticity and be real in my relationship with you and others. May I find comfort in your love and walk in the freedom of knowing that I am cherished for who I truly am. In Jesus' name, I pray. Amen.

Daily Reflection:

God loves your authenticity so much that HE considers you deserving of sacrificing His only son and promised eternal life if you believe in Him.

2

EMBRACING AUTHENTICITY: GOD'S VIEW OF YOU

Scripture:

> *"He said to me, 'I am going to make you fruitful and increase your numbers. I will make you a community of peoples, and I will give this land as an everlasting possession to your descendants after you"* **Genesis 48:4** (NIV).

Devotional

God has the best plan for all His children, and He is capable and willing to give us all the resources we need to be fruitful.

In the sacred pages of Genesis 48:4, we find a profound message about how God view us as authentic beings. This verse is not just a promise given to Joseph by his father, Jacob, but it also reveals a deep truth about the way God sees us and values the authenticity in each of us.

In this passage, Jacob, also known as Israel, was speaking to his son Joseph. He blessed him and affirmed God's promises over his life. The words he utters resonate with a powerful message for all of God's children. Let's unpack the significance of this verse and explore how it reflects God's view of our authenticity.

1. God's Intention for Fruitfulness:

God has good intentions for us. Jacob's declaration to his son, saying, "*I am going to make you fruitful,*" also echoes God's heart and intention for each one of us. God desires to see us bear fruit in our lives. This fruitfulness extends beyond material abundance but also about producing the fruit of the Spirit: love, joy, peace, patience, kindness, goodness, faithfulness, gentleness, and self-control (Galatians 5:22-23). As we embrace our authenticity and draw closer to God, we become vessels through which His fruit can be manifest in our lives.

2. Embracing Your Unique Identity:

"*I will make you a community of peoples.*" God created you with a unique identity, a distinct purpose, and a special role to play in His grand plan. Do you recall that the Bible says He knew your name even before you were formed in the womb? This is an affirmation of God's intimate knowledge and purposeful design for you. He sees the beauty in your individuality and longs for you to embrace your authentic self. The body of Christ is a diverse and dynamic community, and God values each member's contribution. Your authenticity, your story, and your gifts are an essential part of this tapestry.

3. An Everlasting Possession:

"*I will give this land as an everlasting possession to your descendants after you.*" God's promise of an everlasting possession reflects His commitment to you and your legacy. Just as He made an eternal covenant with the patriarchs, He extends His everlasting love and favour to you. Your authenticity is a cornerstone of that legacy passed down to future generations as a testimony of God's faithfulness.

As you reflect on Genesis 48:4, remember that God not only sees you but deeply values your authenticity. Your unique experiences, talents, and quirks are all part of His grand design. Just as Joseph received the blessing of fruitfulness, community, and an everlasting possession, God desires to lavish His blessings upon you. As you walk in the authenticity of who He created you to be, you are opening yourself to receive the countless blessings He has prepared for you.

Prayer:

Heavenly Father,

We thank You for the way You view us as authentic and

valuable individuals. Help us to fully embrace our uniqueness and recognise that our authenticity is a reflection of Your divine craftsmanship. May we bear the fruits of the Spirit, contribute to the community of faith, and leave a lasting legacy in Jesus' name, we pray. Amen.

Daily Reflection:

God values your authenticity and desires to bless you with fruitfulness, increase, community, and an everlasting legacy.

3

EMBRACING GOD'S AUTHENTIC PERSPECTIVE

Scripture:

> "*Even though I walk through the darkest valley, I will fear no evil, for you are with me; your rod and your staff, they comfort me*" **Psalm 23:4** (NIV).

Devotional

We find assurance of protection from God alone.

In our journey through life, we often face moments of uncertainty, doubt, and fear. The path may take us through dark valleys, where the shadows of our insecurities and doubts loom large. In such moments, it is easy to lose sight of who we truly are and question our worth and authenticity. But the beautiful truth is that God, our loving Shepherd, sees us in an entirely different light.

Psalm 23:4 assures us of God's unwavering presence and guidance in the midst of life's trials. Even when we walk through the darkest valleys, we need not fear, for God is with us. His rod and staff provide comfort and protection. This verse reveals a profound aspect of God's perspective on us: He sees us as authentic, cherished, and unconditionally loved, no matter the circumstances.

Think of Daniel in the lion's den. All he did was pray to God as he usually did, and he was thrown into the den for the lions to devour, but God protected him by ensuring those lions weren't hungry until Daniel was released. That's the power of God's presence over His children. An that moment, Daniel could have sworn that God had forsaken him, but he chose to trust in God's unfailing love for his children.

God's rod represents His authority and power, while His staff symbolises His gentle care and guidance. In this combination, we find a balance that perfectly complements our authentic selves. God's authority doesn't stifle our uniqueness, but rather, it empowers us to live authentically. His gentle care doesn't condemn or criticise our imperfections but rather lovingly nudges us toward growth and transformation.

Just as a shepherd knows each sheep in their flock, God intimately knows us. He knows every facet of our being, every joy and every sorrow. He knows the dreams we hold deep in our hearts and the fears that keep us awake at night. Yet, in His eyes, we are still valued and cherished. He doesn't see our mistakes or flaws as barriers to His love. Instead, He sees opportunities for His grace and mercy to shine through.

When you feel like an imposter or are overwhelmed by the world's expectations, remember that God's perspective is radically different; you are unique and created in His image. Embrace your authentic self, knowing that God has a divine purpose for your life, even in the darkest valleys, when situations around seem to say otherwise. Let His presence bring you comfort, peace, and the assurance of your true worth.

Prayer:

Heavenly Father,

Thank you for seeing me as I truly am and for knowing me in a way that no one else can. When I doubt my worth and authenticity, help me to remember that you are my Shepherd, guiding me with love and care. In the darkest valleys of life, may I fear no evil, for you are with me. Your rod and staff bring comfort and assurance.

Grant me the strength to embrace my authentic self, to walk confidently in the path you've set before me, and to live in the fullness of your love and purpose. Let your perspective be the foundation of my identity, and may I find peace in knowing that I am cherished and loved by you. Amen.

Daily Reflection:

Let God's unwavering presence and guidance assure you of your uniqueness and authenticity, even in life's darkest valleys.

4

EMBRACING GOD'S AUTHENTIC LOVE

Scripture:

> "*And God is able to bless you abundantly so that in all things at all times, having all that you need, you will abound in every good work*" **2 Corinthians 9:8** (NIV).

Devotional

God knows what exactly you need and is capable of providing them all.

In a world where authenticity seems elusive, we often find ourselves wearing masks and hiding behind a facade to fit in, to be accepted, or to meet the expectations of others. The constant pressure to conform can lead us to believe that we need to behave in a certain kind of way or become someone else other than our true selves. But the Word of God reminds us that we are seen differently in His eyes.

In 2 Corinthians 9:8, we find a beautiful promise that speaks directly to the heart of our authenticity. It says, "And God is able to bless you abundantly so that in all things at all times, having all that you need, you will abound in every good work."

This verse reveals a profound truth about God's perspective on us. He knows us intimately, and His love for us is not based on any pretence or performance. God sees you for who you truly are and loves you with authentic, unwavering love. You are His masterpiece, created with unique talents, passions, and a purpose that only you can fulfil.

We can take comfort in knowing that God doesn't require us to be something we're not. Instead, He blesses us abundantly, not because of our perfection, but because of His love and grace. His blessings flow to us, not when we hide behind a mask, but when we embrace our true selves. In His love, we find the freedom to be authentic.

David is a good example of someone whom the world would naturally condemn, but God saw more than a flawed man. He saw someone who was authentic enough to fail, feel remorse for his mistakes, and still run back to God for help. God loves it when we come to him as we are, not as we think we should be.

Regardless of what the world has said about us and what we

think about ourselves, God will never condemn us; rather, he gives us grace and allows us to see through his lens and accept our new identity in Christ.

As you reflect on this promise, remember that God's authenticity toward you calls you to embrace your authenticity before Him. He desires a relationship with the real you, flaws and all. When you come to Him in your vulnerability, He can work through you in ways you never thought possible.

Prayer:

Heavenly Father,

Thank you for your abundant love and grace. We are grateful that you see us for who we truly are and that you love us authentically. Help us, Lord, to let go of the masks we hide under and to be our true selves before you. Empower us to walk confidently in the authenticity of your love, knowing that we are accepted and cherished just as we are.

Grant us the courage to embrace our uniqueness and to live out the purpose you've designed for us. May we abound in every good work, not through our own strength, but through your divine blessing and guidance. Amen.

Daily Reflection:

Consider how God's abundant blessings validate your authenticity, calling you to embrace your true self and rely on His unending grace.

5
EMBRACING GOD'S AUTHENTIC VISION FOR YOU

Scripture:

> *"His divine power has given us everything we need for a godly life through our knowledge of him who called us by his own glory and goodness"* **2 Peter 1:3** (NIV).

Devotional

God knows the beginning and ending of your story.

In a world that often encourages us to be a certain way or follow standards set by fellow human beings, losing sight of our authenticity can be very easy. The pressures of bowing to society and the desire to fit in can lead us to put on fake personalities, leaving our true selves hidden. But today, we want to remind you of the beautiful truth found in 2 Peter 1:3: God sees you as authentic.

God's divine power has equipped us with everything we need for a life of godliness. This includes not just external actions but the very core of who we are - our authenticity. In other words, our authenticity is part of the 'everything' needed for godliness. God calls us to be authentic because He knows us intimately and created us uniquely for a specific purpose. God's vision for you is not to become a copy of someone else or to conform to the world's expectations but for you to embrace your true self – the person He lovingly crafted.

When God looks at you, He sees beyond the exterior. He sees your heart, desires, strengths, and weaknesses. He knows your struggles, and He still loves you just the way you are. His glory and goodness called you, and His divine power empowers you to be the authentic person He intended you to be.

Think of Saul, who later became Paul. People hated him because they had a bad experience with him, but when God changed his life, he didn't let that stop him from accepting his new identity. He didn't try to please the old him or get scared of being condemned.

You don't need to pretend or hide anymore. God's acceptance is not based on your performance or the opinions of others. His acceptance is based on His unconditional love for you. He delights in your authenticity because when you are authentic, you reflect

His glory and goodness in a unique way that no one else can.

Prayer:

Heavenly Father,

We thank You for seeing us as authentic and loving us just as we are. Help us to embrace the beautiful truth that You have given us everything we need for a godly life, including the strength to be our authentic selves. Release us from the bondage of pretence and fear of judgement. May we live in the freedom of Your acceptance, knowing that we are fearfully and wonderfully made in Your image. As we walk in our authenticity, may we bring glory to Your name and touch the lives of those around us. In Jesus' name, we pray. Amen.

Daily Reflection:

God's divine power is what enables you to live authentically and to fulfil the purpose He crafted for you.

6
EMBRACING YOUR AUTHENTIC SELF IN GOD'S EYES

Scripture:

> *"Then the Lord was jealous for his land and took pity on his people. The Lord replied to them: 'I am sending you grain, new wine and olive oil, enough to satisfy you fully; never again will I make you an object of scorn to the nations"* **Joel 2:18-19** (NIV).

Devotional

Have you ever seen a good father leave his children to suffer?

Remaining steadfast, authentic and true to one's self can be a challenge amid constant pressures, struggles, expectations, and aspirations we strive to achieve. We often find ourselves striving to meet the standards set by society, friends, or even our own self-criticism. In this struggle to fit in, we may forget how God truly sees us. The book of Joel, especially in the verses from Joel 2:18-19, offers a powerful reminder of God's perspective on our authenticity.

Joel's words were written to a people who had turned away from God and faced the consequences of their actions. Yet, God's response is not one of judgement and rejection but of compassion and restoration. The Lord was "jealous of his land", desiring to reclaim His people and show them His abundant grace.

God's view of you is filled with love and compassion. He sees past the masks we often wear to fit in or hide our imperfections. In His eyes, you are His cherished creation, fearfully and wonderfully made. God's desire is not for you to be an imitation of someone else but to embrace your authentic self.

In the same way that the Lord promised to provide grain, new wine, and olive oil in abundance, He desires to satisfy your deepest needs. God's provisions go beyond physical sustenance; they encompass the longing of your heart for belonging, purpose, and authenticity. When you allow God to work in your life, you become a living testament to His love and grace, and you will not be an object of scorn to the world.

So, let us take a moment to reflect on our own lives. Are we striving to be someone we are not, or are we willing to embrace the authentic self that God created? As you seek to be your true self, remember that God sees you with eyes of love and approval. Your authenticity brings joy to His heart.

Prayer:

Heavenly Father,

Thank you for seeing us as we truly are, for loving us despite our imperfections, and for desiring our authenticity. Help us, Lord, to let go of the masks and pretences that we often wear and to be our true selves in your presence. Fill us with your grace and love so that we may shine as a beacon of your authenticity in a world filled with expectations.

As we strive to live in the fullness of your love, may our lives be a testimony to the transformation you bring. We pray for the strength to be genuine in our faith, relationships, and daily lives. May your blessings, like the abundance of grain, new wine, and olive oil, flow into our lives and satisfy our every need. In Jesus' name, we pray. Amen

Daily Reflection:

Remember that God's love and compassion beckon you to embrace your authenticity, and to trust in His abundant provision to meet your deepest needs.

7

EMBRACING AUTHENTICITY THROUGH SPIRITUAL BLESSINGS

Scripture:

> *"Blessed be the God and Father of our Lord Jesus Christ, who has blessed us with every spiritual blessing in the heavenly places in Christ"* **Ephesians 1:3** (NKJV).

Devotional

If you don't know what you possess, you will think you are empty.

Have you ever felt a sense of disconnection in your life? As if something was missing, despite the blessings that surround you? It's not uncommon to long for a deeper understanding of who we are and what our purpose in life is. Thankfully, in Ephesians 1:3, we discover a powerful truth that can lead us to find our authenticity.

God, our Heavenly Father, has blessed us "with every spiritual blessing in the heavenly places in Christ." These blessings are not external, temporary, or materialistic; rather, they come from the depths of our souls. They are the keys to unlocking the door to our authentic selves.

Embracing our authenticity begins with recognising that we are children of God, chosen and loved by Him. Despite our flaws and imperfections, God accepts us just as we are. His love for us is unchanging, unwavering, and unconditional. When we understand and embrace this truth, we can let go of the masks we wear and the insecurities that hold us back.

Finding our authenticity also requires us to walk in the spiritual blessings that God has already placed within us. Often, it is easy to look outwardly for validation and acceptance, seeking fulfilment in achievements, possessions, or the opinions of others. However, our true fulfilment lies in the spiritual blessings bestowed upon us by Christ.

For us to identify and use these gifts right, we need to submit to God, know who we are in him and allow him to guide us.

These spiritual blessings include love, joy, peace, patience, kindness, goodness, faithfulness, gentleness, and self-control (Galatians 5:22-23). As we allow these blessings to manifest in our lives, we begin to discover our true selves — the unique individuals God created us to be. We no longer need to look to others for validation because we understand that our true worth comes from our identity in Christ.

Finally, as we come to grasp our authenticity, we can fully embrace our purpose in God's kingdom. Each of us has a unique calling, talents, and gifts that are meant to be used for His glory. When our authentic selves align with God's plan for our lives, we can impact the world in profound and meaningful ways.

Prayer:

Heavenly Father,

Thank You for the spiritual blessings You have lavished upon me in Christ. Help me to understand and embrace my true authenticity, accepting who I am in Your eyes. I release the insecurities and masks that have hindered me from living authentically. Fill me with Your love and empower me to walk in the spiritual blessings You have placed within me. Guide me along the path of my purpose and grant me the courage to impact the world as the unique individual You created me to be. In Jesus' name, I pray. Amen.

Daily Reflection:

Recognising your spiritual blessings in Christ and embracing your true self allows you to find authentic fulfilment and purpose in God's plan for your life.

8

UNLEASHING AUTHENTICITY THROUGH GOD'S EMPOWERMENT

Scripture:

> "*Now to Him who is able to do immeasurably more than all we ask or imagine, according to His power that is at work within us*" **Ephesians 3:20** (NIV).

Devotional

Dear beloved, have you ever felt like you were living a life that didn't truly reflect who you are at the core? Sometimes, we find ourselves caught up in societal expectations, trying to please others or disguising ourselves under the mask of conformity. But today, let us delve into an inspiring verse from Ephesians 3:20 and learn how it can anchor our souls, guiding us towards a path of authenticity in everything we do.

At first glance, this verse may appear unrelated to the

pursuit of authenticity. However, as we deeply reflect upon it, we come to realise that unveiling our true selves requires tapping into the power of God that resides within us.

God, the creator of the universe, has endowed us with unique gifts, talents, and passions. He has woven our very essence into the tapestry of creation, and we are fearfully and wonderfully made in His image (Psalm 139:14). Yet, often, we hide our true selves, fearing rejection and judgement.

When Jesus came to the world, He didn't try to be like others. Other than coming in the form of a human, He didn't try to make His message suitable for all or try to pet anyone's ego; He delivered it as authentically as he should; that's exactly how God wants us to be our true selves, even if it means being the only light in the dark. That's God's gift to us, and we need to showcase it to fulfil our purpose.

Authenticity comes when we align our hearts, minds, and actions with the purpose God has placed within us. It is through embracing this divine purpose and allowing God's power to work within us that we discover our true potential and fulfilment.

When we attempt to live inauthentically, we limit ourselves and hinder our journey towards growth and true joy. However, when we surrender to God's power within us, we open doors to a life beyond our own imagination.

Let us be encouraged to let go of the masks we wear and the limitations we impose upon ourselves. Instead, let us boldly step forward with confidence, knowing that God's strength and grace will pave the way for unfathomable growth and unimaginable possibilities.

Prayer:

Dear Heavenly Father,

Thank you for creating me in Your image and for instilling in me a unique purpose. I surrender my fears, insecurities, and doubts at Your feet today. I choose to step into the authenticity that You have placed within me.

Help me to embrace the power of Your Holy Spirit, which guides me towards a life overflowing with truth, purpose, and genuine joy. Strengthen me when doubt creeps in and remind me of Your promise to do immeasurably more than I could ask or imagine.

Lord, as I embark on this journey of authenticity, grant me the courage to break free from societal expectations, cast aside the masks I wear, and pursue the life You have deeply whispered into my soul. Empower me to be a vessel of love, truth, and light in this world. In Jesus' name, I pray. Amen.

Daily Reflection:

Allow God's immeasurable power within you guide your true purpose and endow you with the capacity to embrace your true self.

9

EMBRACING MY AUTHENTIC SELF AS GOD'S IMAGE

Scripture:

> *"Then God said, 'Let us make mankind in our image, in our likeness, so that they may rule over the fish in the sea and the birds in the sky, over the livestock and all the wild animals, and over all the creatures that move along the ground.' So God created mankind in his own image, in the image of God he created them; male and female he created them. God blessed them and said to them, 'Be fruitful and increase in number; fill the earth and subdue it. Rule over the fish in the sea and the birds in the sky and over every living creature that moves on the ground'"* **Genesis 1:26-28** (NIV).

Devotional

It's easy to lose sight of our true selves in today's world because we all want to look the same; we want to look like someone that we picture as perfection. However, as children of God, our identity is rooted in His infinite wisdom and love. It is through the profound words in Genesis 1:26-28 that we discover the path to embracing our authentic selves.

As we delve into these verses, let us first acknowledge that God created us in His own image and likeness. We are unique reflections of His divine attributes and loving nature. This recognition tells us that our identity was never meant to be defined by the world but rather by our Creator. In a broken and imperfect world, we are still called to shine His light by embracing our true selves.

It's a blessing to be made in God's image and be entrusted with the responsibility of expanding God's kingdom. Nobody's opinion of us should be greater than that which our maker has of us. When we remind ourselves of the privilege we enjoy, we won't be fazed by what others do.

Through this passage, we also see that God blessed mankind and gave them authority over His creation. This signifies that we possess a great purpose and responsibility. By living out our authentic selves, we can effectively fulfil this purpose and impact the world. We unlock our potential to make a difference and reflect God's character when we step into our true identity.

Finding our authenticity requires unearthing the unique combination of talents, passions, and qualities God has woven into our being. It involves discovering our God-given purpose and allowing it to guide every aspect of our lives. We must engage in sincere introspection, seeking God's guidance and embracing the gifts He has bestowed upon us. By drawing near to Him, we find the strength and courage to be the person God created us to be.

Prayer:

Gracious Father,

Thank You for creating me in Your image and likeness. Help me to embrace my true identity as Your child. As I reflect upon Genesis 1:26-28, may I find wisdom and strength to live authentically - revealing the unique attributes You have endowed me with. Guide me on this journey, Lord, as I navigate through the many influences that attempt to shape me. Grant me the courage to be my true self, shining your light wherever I go. In Jesus' name, I pray. Amen.

Daily Reflection:

Your ability to recognise that you are God's special creature, made in His image, and entrusted with His other creations will propel you to discover your true self and embrace your divine authenticity and identity.

10

EMBRACING AUTHENTICITY THROUGH FAITH

Scripture:

> "*For this is what the Lord says: You will see neither wind nor rain, yet this valley will be filled with water, and you, your cattle, and your other animals will drink*" **2 Kings 3:17** (NIV).

Devotional

Staying true to our authentic selves can be challenging in a world that wants us to constantly comply with certain rules and urges us to fit into predefined patterns. We often find ourselves contending with societal expectations, comparisons, and the fear of judgement, causing us to conceal our true selves. But as we seek to find our identity, God's Word reminds us that authenticity is not only possible; it is essential.

The passage in 2 Kings 3:17 presents a powerful image of

God's promise to the people of Israel. In the context of a drought-stricken land, the Lord assures them that the valley will be filled with water even without any visible sign of rain or wind. This account teaches us an invaluable lesson about authenticity and finding our true selves in God.

Just as God fulfils His promise to provide water without the normal signs, He calls us to be true to ourselves in a world that may not always understand or appreciate our uniqueness. It is a divine reassurance that our authenticity lies not in conforming to societal norms but in embracing the unique characteristics, talents, and passions that God has bestowed upon us.

When you think about how the world adopts worldly practices, you will find it hard to believe that your voice will be heard, let alone that you will win souls for Christ, but remember that the God that brings water out of the desert can touch the heart of men to receive His Word. So do your part, believe, and let God do His part the way He wants.

You believe that God parted the sea without witnessing it yourself, so serve God knowing that you don't have to understand everything, the same way people don't have to agree with your choice to serve God.

Finding our authenticity begins with acknowledging that God has crafted each of us with a specific purpose and calling in mind. We are fearfully and wonderfully made in His image (Psalm 139:14), and our true identity lies in yielding our lives to reflect His glory. When we align our thoughts, actions, and desires with God's will, we begin to live authentically.

However, the journey toward authenticity may not be easy. We might face moments of doubt, insecurity, or rejection, but remember that God's promises endure forever. His faithfulness will fill the emptiness within us, refreshing our spirits and emboldening us to stand firm in who we are in Christ.

Remember, dear friend, embracing your authenticity in Christ will let you experience a deeper sense of fulfilment and also inspire and encourage others to do the same. Stay true to who you are, for that is where God's blessings await you.

Prayer:

Dear Heavenly Father,

Thank you for reminding us of Your promises and the value of our authenticity. We come before You boldly, seeking Your guidance and strength to walk in authenticity. Guide us as we navigate a world that often tries to shape us into its mould. Help us to embrace the unique qualities You have given us, and empower us to honour You through them. Grant us the courage to be our genuine selves, allowing Your light to shine through us for the sake of Your Kingdom. In the name of Jesus, we pray. Amen.

Daily Reflection:

Will you trust Go solely, even when it doesn't make sense? Just as God filled the valley with water despite no visible signs of rain, He calls us to embrace our true selves, trusting His unique purpose for us even when the world doesn't understand.

11
EMBRACING AUTHENTICITY THROUGH CONFIDENCE

Scripture:

> *"Therefore, do not throw away your confidence, which has a great reward"* **Hebrews 10:35** (ESV).

Devotional

We tend to belittle our skills and person, especially when we focus our minds on the world's standards, thereby seeking validation from others. However, as believers, we are called to live a life marked by authenticity. But how do we discover and embrace our true selves?

Hebrews 10:35 provides us with a powerful reminder: "Therefore, do not throw away your confidence, which has a great reward." This verse holds the key to finding our authenticity and living in the joy of who God created us to be.

When we read this verse, the author of Hebrews encourages us not to discard our confidence. Confidence here doesn't refer to worldly arrogance or self-centeredness but rather a confidence rooted in our relationship with Jesus Christ. It is the type of confidence found in knowing that we are fearfully and wonderfully made (Psalm 139:14) and deeply loved by our Heavenly Father.

Authenticity begins with acknowledging that our worth is not based on what the world says about us or what we achieve but on who we are in Christ. As we fully grasp this truth, we can begin to peel away the layers of insecurity, fear, and comparison that hinder us from embracing our authentic selves.

God wants us to embrace our unique selves with confidence in His Words to the point that people around us will want to be like us; He wants us to be proud of who we are as His children.

This process of discovering authenticity involves being honest with ourselves and God. It doesn't mean that we need to have everything figured out or that we need to be perfect. Instead, it requires vulnerability and surrendering our flaws, weaknesses, and doubts to the Lord.

As we cultivate a deeper relationship with God, spending time in His presence and studying His Word, He gently uncovers our true identity. Through His guidance and the work of His Holy Spirit within us, we begin to see ourselves as He sees us - as cherished, forgiven, and accepted children of God.

Walking in authenticity often requires us to let go of the need for approval or acceptance from others. It means embracing our unique abilities, quirks, and passions, knowing that God created each aspect of our being with purpose. When we learn to love and accept ourselves as God does, others' opinions have no power over us.

Prayer:

Heavenly Father,

Thank You for reminding me that my true worth and confidence lie in my relationship with You. Help me to embrace my authentic self, free from the pressure to conform to the world's standards. Take away any doubts, fears, or insecurities within me, and fill me with Your love and acceptance. Guide me in my journey of discovering who You created me to be and help me to unashamedly embrace my unique identity. Strengthen me to walk boldly in the path You have set before me, knowing that my identity is securely rooted in Christ alone. In Jesus' name, I pray. Amen.

Daily Reflection:

With your head up high, confidently embrace your true identity in Christ and live authentically, free from external validations.

12
EMBRACING AUTHENTICITY IN GOD'S EYES

Scripture:

> *"Being confident of this, that he who began a good work in you will carry it on to completion until the day of Christ Jesus"* **Philippians 1:6** (NIV).

Devotional

God never leaves any project unfinished; if you are still alive, it means He's still working on your story.

The world shows us only the good side of things and how fast people are making it, and while we consume this content, we tend to be impatient and doubtful of God's timing and promise. However, as we reflect on Philippians 1:6, we find assurance and comfort in God's perspective of us.

This also reminds us that the journey to authenticity is impossible without God riding along with us.

The Apostle Paul's words in this scripture remind us that God has initiated a good work in each of us. He started a divine masterpiece within us that reflects His image. In God's eyes, you are uniquely authentic, and He desires to see that authenticity shine through.

God doesn't want us to pretend to be something we're not or to conform to the world's standards. He sees us for who we truly are and loves us unconditionally. Our journey toward authenticity is not a solo endeavour; it's a partnership with God.

When we allow God to work in our lives, He continually refines us, shapes us, and guides us toward a more authentic self. He knows the real you, the one He created with love, purpose, and uniqueness. God sees your potential, and He is committed to seeing that potential fully realised.

Authenticity, in God's eyes, means being true to the person He designed you to be. It's about embracing your strengths and weaknesses, your gifts and talents, and your quirks and idiosyncrasies. You don't need to change your perception of yourself, struggle to fit in or feel like anyone else because you are fearfully and wonderfully made by the Creator of the universe.

God has never delivered anything late; He is always right on time, just the same way Jesus raised Lazarus to life after two days. *To us, He might be late, but to God, it was the right time!*

Prayer:

Dear Heavenly Father,

We come before You with gratitude in our hearts for the work you have begun in us. We thank you for creating us in Your image and for the uniqueness that makes us authentic. Lord, sometimes we struggle to be ourselves in a world where we are pressured to conform. Help us to remember that You see us for who we truly are and love us just as we are.

May we have the confidence to be authentic in Your eyes, embracing our strengths and acknowledging our weaknesses. We trust that the work You've started with us will be completed in Your perfect time. We surrender ourselves to Your guidance, knowing that Your plan for our authenticity is far better than any worldly standard.

Thank You for the assurance we find in Philippians 1:6, reminding us of Your commitment to our growth and transformation. We pray for the strength to be true to ourselves, confident in Your love, and eager to reflect Your image to the world.

In Jesus' name, we pray. Amen.

Daily Reflection:

You are God's masterpiece; His ongoing work within you is a journey towards authentic self-realisation, and He will faithfully perfect it.

13

GOD'S UNWAVERING VIEW OF YOUR AUTHENTIC SELF

Scripture:

> "*Your eyes saw my unformed body; all the days ordained for me were written in your book before one of them came to be*" **Psalm 139:16** (NIV).

Devotional

God is the author of your story, so He knows what will happen next in your life and what you will become. When He sees a heart surrender to Him, He beautifies such life/story.

We must be assured that the acts and scenes in our life stories are all known by God. Without this assurance, we'll always be tempted to peep into other people's stories, compare them with ours, and covet something similar because theirs look interesting. But, as believers, we must remember that God sees us differently. He sees us as authentic beings, created purposefully, wonderfully and fearfully in His image. He also has unique stories for all of us.

Psalm 139 is a beautiful reminder of God's intimate knowledge of us. He knows our thoughts, our actions, and our deepest desires. He even knew us before we were formed in the womb. The Creator of the universe took the time to carefully craft every detail of our being, from our physical appearance to our unique personalities. He did this with a purpose in mind, and that purpose is to fulfil His divine plan for our lives.

God doesn't see us as mere imitations of someone else or as people striving to meet human expectations. Instead, He sees us as His beloved children, each with a distinct purpose and calling. He sees the authentic you–the person He designed you to be.

Embracing your authentic self is a journey that requires trust in God's design. It involves letting go of the need for approval from others and seeking affirmation from the One who formed you. Remember that God's view of you is unwavering, and His love for you is unconditional. He is not disappointed in your authentic self; He rejoices in it.

As you reflect on Psalm 139:16, take a moment to pray and seek God's guidance in fully embracing your authentic self.

Prayer:

Dear Heavenly Father,

I come before You with a heart filled with gratitude for the way. You have fearfully and wonderfully made me. Thank You for seeing me as I truly am, for knowing every detail of my being, and for having a purpose for my life. Help me, Lord, to embrace my authentic self and let go of the need for approval from the world. I pray for the courage to walk in the path You've designed for me, trusting in Your plan and love.

May I be a living testimony of Your grace and love as I live out the unique purpose You've written for me. Thank you for your unwavering view of me, and may I seek to align myself with Your perspective every day. In Jesus' name, I pray. Amen.

Daily Reflection:

Never doubt God's unwavering love for you. He created you wonderfully and fearfully in His image, and He has ordained your days on earth with a unique and divine purpose.

14

EMBRACING AUTHENTICITY OPENLY AND PRIVATELY

Scripture:

> *"For there is nothing hidden that will not be disclosed, and nothing concealed that will not be known or brought out into the open"* **Luke 8:17** (NIV).

Devotional

Every event, individual or moment we experience in our lives is known to God, and so the things we think we do in secret are known to God even before we do them. He is Omnipresent.

In the eyes of God, authenticity holds immense value. The words of Luke echo the profound truth that everything concealed will eventually be revealed. This truth extends beyond mere actions; it delves into the core of our being, our authenticity.

On judgement day, everything we have done will be shown

to us, so why don't we live a life that we will be proud of when we stand in front of our Lord on the final day? We should stop acting for the camera while having skeletons in our cupboards and thinking God isn't aware. We would be deceiving ourselves, and in the end, the consequence of that deceitful life would fall on us and wreck us.

God does not see you the way you present yourself to the world but as the sum of your thoughts, emotions, and intentions. He sees the authenticity of your heart, the parts hidden or concealed from the world, and in His eyes, there's an immense appreciation for your genuine self.

Authenticity is a journey—a journey to embrace your true self and align your thoughts, actions, and beliefs. It's about being genuine, transparent, and honest with yourself and with others. In a world that often celebrates pretence, God calls us to embrace our true identity and live authentically.

When you open your heart to God, you invite Him into every aspect of your being. There's no need to hide or pretend because God sees beyond the facade. He loves you unconditionally and embraces the real you, imperfections and all. His love is not based on your performance or appearance but on the authenticity of your heart.

Prayer:

Dear God,

Thank You for seeing me as I truly am and for embracing my authenticity. Help me to walk in honesty and truth, aligning my thoughts and actions with Your will. Grant me the courage to be genuine in a world that often encourages conformity. Strengthen me to live authentically, reflecting Your love and truth in all I do.

Let me find peace and strength in the assurance that You cherish my authenticity and love me just as I am. In Your loving name, Amen.

Daily Reflection:

Why living a two-faced life? Why the double/multiple identity? Come to Hod with an open heart; He knows you more than you know yourself.

15
LIVING AUTHENTICALLY: EMBRACING TRUTH

Scripture:

> "*Therefore, each of you must put off falsehood and speak truthfully to your neighbour, for we are all members of one body*" **Ephesians 4:25** (NIV).

Devotional

We all want to associate with sincere people because we seek trust and security when sharing bits of our lives with others. But then it starts with. As the bible says, before we pick the dirt in someone else's eyes, we should pick ours first.

So ask yourself, "Am I a sincere person? Can people trust me?"

In the tapestry of life, authenticity weaves the threads of genuine connections and sincere relationships. Ephesians

4:25 stands as a beacon, calling for honesty and transparency in our interactions.

God wants us to show a Christlike life in our interaction with people in the world, letting off malice, gossip, lies and healthy conversations that don't propagate the gospel. We should be easily identified as children of God in our relationships and conversations.

Authenticity isn't merely a personal virtue but a communal responsibility. This verse, penned by the apostle Paul, echoes the importance of truth-telling within the fabric of the Christian community. It implores us to discard the cloak of deceit and embrace the liberating power of truthfulness.

Living authentically demands courage. It beckons us to peel away the layers of pretence, revealing our true selves. In a world often adorned with masks, being authentic is a revolutionary act—an act that honours our shared humanity and interconnectedness.

This verse serves as a compass, guiding us towards sincerity in our words and actions. It encourages us to step into vulnerability, understanding that it's in our authenticity that genuine connections flourish. The goal and purpose of life is to please God, and so when we begin to say what God hasn't said or put down others with our words, we are depopulating the kingdom and giving a false narrative of what Christianity is.

In the tapestry of faith, our authenticity colours the intricate patterns of fellowship. Let us, therefore, embrace Ephesians 4:25 as a call to authenticity—a call to speak truthfully, live sincerely, and nurture a community that thrives on the beauty of honesty.

Prayer:

Gracious God,

Help me embrace authenticity in every corner of my life. Grant me the audacity to speak truthfully and the wisdom to live authentically. May my authenticity serve as a testament to Your love and grace, fostering deeper connections within my community. In Jesus' name, amen.

Daily Reflection:

How truthful are you living your life and embracing your authenticity? God sees and knows everything you conceal, so why not bare it all before your Creator?

16

WALKING IN INTEGRITY: A PATHWAY TO AUTHENTIC LIVING

Scripture:

> *"The integrity of the upright guides them, but the unfaithful are destroyed by their duplicity"* **Proverbs 11:3** (NIV).

Devotional

One with integrity is someone who is honest and refuses to throw away their moral principles. The beauty of having integrity is that everyone will feel it through your speech, aura, and way of life or service to others. You can't hide it because it's something that has to be put into practice or something you must always act.

In the labyrinth of life, the compass that directs our steps towards authenticity is integrity. Proverbs 11:3 stands as a steadfast reminder of the profound impact of living a life marked by honesty and sincerity.

Integrity isn't just a moral virtue; it's a guiding light, a moral code that shapes our decisions and actions. This verse, penned by the wise, exhorts us to walk in the path of authenticity. It illuminates the way for the upright, those who choose the journey of integrity.

Authenticity springs from integrity, from the alignment of our inner values with our outward actions. It's a commitment to consistency, where our words resonate with our deeds. Living authentically is a radical choice in a world filled with noise and pretence—it's a commitment to truthfulness, transparency, and wholeness.

Proverbs 11:3 acts as a mirror, reflecting the consequences of living inauthentically. Duplicity corrodes the spirit and fractures relationships. Yet, choosing integrity empowers us to stand firm, unshaken by the allure of deception.

Let this verse be the cornerstone of your pursuit of authenticity. Let it guide your steps, anchoring you in the waters of truthfulness and paving the way for a life that honours God and blesses others.

Prayer:

Gracious Father,

Help me walk in the path of integrity, for in it lies the essence of authenticity. Grant me the strength to uphold honesty and sincerity in all aspects of my life. May my words and actions align with Your truth, illuminating a path of authenticity for others to follow. In Jesus' name, amen.

Daily Reflection:

You have to be a person of integrity to live authentically. Integrity serves as a lantern, illuminating your path and leading you to truth and wholeness.

17

EMBRACING TRUTH: YOUR LIBERATING POWER

Scripture:

> *"Then you will know the truth, and the truth will set you free"* **John 8:32** (NIV).

Devotional

As kids, we made many mistakes, destroyed some things around the house, or made certain decisions behind our parents' backs. When they suspected or found out, they always called us to confirm if it was true or not. In those moments, we sometimes choose to lie because we don't want to be punished or grounded. But the truth is, their questioning didn't mean they were unaware; they wanted to give us a chance to explain and show if the morals they have taught us really have taken root.

Sometimes, we fear the consequences of telling the truth, and we forget that it's worse to tell a lie. The truth will definitely set us free. Sometimes, it comes with a punishment, but it builds trust between us and our parents, and other times, they just let us go with no punishment. God wants the same in our relationship with Him and others, knowing that telling the truth brings peace and freedom from the bondage of guilt.

In the symphony of life, authenticity harmonises with truth. John 8:32 resonates as a profound melody, inviting us to embrace the liberating power of authenticity through truth. Authenticity finds its resonance in truthfulness. This verse, spoken by Jesus, echoes the transformative nature of truth. It's a call to live authentically, liberated from the chains of pretence and falsehood.

Living authentically isn't merely about self-expression; it's about living in alignment with the ultimate truth. It's an acknowledgement that genuine freedom arises from a life steeped in honesty, where our thoughts, words, and actions echo the song of truth.

John 8:32 invites us to shed the masks that conceal our true selves. Authentic living begins with an honest introspection, embracing both our strengths and vulnerabilities. It's in this embrace of truth that we find the freedom to be unapologetically ourselves.

Let this verse be your guiding light towards authenticity. Allow the truth to permeate every facet of your being, leading you towards a life that embraces honesty, integrity, and genuine connections.

Prayer:

Gracious God,

Help me to embrace truth in every aspect of my life. Grant me the courage to live authentically, liberated by the truth You reveal. May my authenticity be a reflection of Your grace and love, inviting others to experience the freedom found in genuine living. In Jesus' name, amen.

Daily Reflection:

True freedom comes from living authentically and embracing the liberating power of truth.

18

DWELLING IN AUTHENTICITY BY LIVING IN INTEGRITY

Scripture:

> *"Lord, who may dwell in your sacred tent? Who may live on your holy mountain? The one whose walk is blameless, who does what is righteous, who speaks the truth from their heart"* **Psalm 15:1-2 (NIV).**

Devotional

In the sacred verses of Psalm 15, authenticity resonates through a life lived in alignment with integrity and righteousness.

This passage beckons us to explore the sanctuary of God's presence by embracing authenticity in our conduct and speech.

Authentic living finds its home in a heart that beats in rhythm with righteousness. As the psalmist ponders, "who may abide in God's presence", the criteria laid out are those of authenticity. It's not about perfection but about a genuine commitment to walk blamelessly, pursue righteousness, and speak truth from the depths of our hearts.

Joseph was a great example of one who lived in integrity. Through the betrayal and hardship, he never for once blamed God or did anything that would stain his pure heart. He was always a man of integrity as a young boy, a prisoner and a prime minister in Egypt.

In **Genesis 50:19-20**, Joseph said to his brothers,

> *"Don't be afraid. Am I in the place of God?; You intended to harm me, but God intended it for good to accomplish what is now being done, the saving of many lives."*

His garment might have been dirty while in the prison, but his heart was as pure as cotton. He would have acted like any human being and cursed his brothers immediately after he saw them or asked the general question, "Why me?" but instead, he forgave them wholeheartedly and brought them to stay with him. He didn't let his circumstances cause him to sleep with Potiphar's wife, hold a grudge or maltreat his brothers.

Through thick and thin, he walked with God and lived a blameless life.

Living authentically is not about outward appearances; it's a reflection of the heart's posture. It's a journey where our actions and words align with the truth that resides within us. This authenticity, rooted in righteousness and truthfulness, invites us into deeper communion with the Divine.

Psalm 15:1-2 is an invitation to introspection, encouraging us to assess the authenticity of our walk, actions, and speech. It inspires us to cultivate a heart that beats in tune with God's truth, paving the way for a life marked by authenticity.

Let this passage be a guiding star in your pursuit of authenticity. May your walk be blameless, your actions righteous, and your speech overflow with truthfulness, creating a dwelling place for God's presence within you.

Prayer:

Heavenly Father,

Grant me the grace to live authentically in Your sight. Help me align my actions and words with the authenticity of Your truth. May my life reflect integrity, righteousness, and truthfulness, inviting Your presence to dwell within me. In Jesus' name, amen.

Daily Reflection:

Living authentically means aligning our actions, words, and heart with righteousness and truth, and living our lives to honour God's presence.

19

AUTHENTIC WISDOM: THE FOUNDATION OF AUTHENTIC LIVING

Scripture:

> "*The fear of the Lord is the beginning of knowledge, but fools despise wisdom and instruction*" **Proverbs 1:7** (NIV).

Devotional

Without wisdom, it's difficult to live a life of understanding God's Words and patterns.

In the tapestry of life, authenticity finds its foundation in the pursuit of wisdom rooted in reverence for the Divine. Proverbs 1:7 resonates as a guiding principle, highlighting the significance of embracing wisdom as a cornerstone of authentic living.

Authenticity isn't just about being true to oneself; it's also about embracing a humble learning posture. This verse, penned by the wise, underscores the importance of the fear of the Lord as the genesis of authentic knowledge. It's an invitation to recognise our limited understanding and seek wisdom from a place of reverence.

Solomon's wisdom began when he decided to offer a thousand burnt offerings to God. Why? Because he wanted God's attention, he needed something from God and knew how to capture God's attention.

And when he finally got God's attention, he didn't ask for riches but asked for wisdom and understanding to rule. A rare request, right? (1 Kings 3:4-28).

Solomon knew he needed wisdom to be an exceptional ruler, and we see how he demonstrated divine wisdom in the case of the two women who claimed one child as theirs. He said that the child be cut into two so each mother could take half, but the real mother refused and asked that the child be given to the other woman.

A real mother will never let her child die, and it was God's wisdom that made him address the issue that way. (1 Kings 3:16-28)

His human mind wouldn't have been able to judge the matter perfectly.

Living authentically involves embracing the wisdom that emanates from honouring God. It's a recognition that true wisdom isn't found in self-assurance but in acknowledging our need for divine guidance and instruction. Authentic living begins with an open heart receptive to wisdom, not with a haughty spirit that rejects counsel.

Proverbs 1:7 serves as a compass, guiding us towards authentic living by acknowledging the source of true wisdom. It invites us to humble ourselves before God, embracing His wisdom and instruction as foundational to our journey.

Let this verse be a guiding light on your path to authenticity. May your pursuit of wisdom, rooted in reverence for the Divine, shape your character and guide your actions, leading to a life that authentically honours God.

Prayer:

Gracious God,

Grant me the humility to seek Your wisdom as the foundation of authentic living. Help me embrace the fear of the Lord as the beginning of knowledge. May Your wisdom guide my steps, shaping me into an authentic reflection of Your grace and truth. In Jesus' name, amen.

Daily Reflection:

Wisdom comes from hearing and obeying God's command. You need wisdom to live authentically.

20

EMBRACING AUTHENTICITY BY PURSUING TRUTH IN GOD

Scripture:

> "*Yet you desired faithfulness even in the womb; you taught me wisdom in that secret place*" **Psalm 51:6** (NIV).

Devotional

In the quiet whispers of Psalm 51, authenticity reverberates through the pursuit of truth and wisdom. This verse unveils a profound truth: God desires authenticity from the very core of our beings, teaching us wisdom even in the hidden recesses of our existence.

Authenticity is not a mere external display but an internal posture, deeply ingrained within us from the very beginning. This verse, penned by David in a moment of heartfelt repentance, reveals God's desire for sincerity and truthfulness rooted in our innermost being.

David was a man after God's heart, not because he was perfect but because every single time he erred, he would confess his sins and ask God for help. He knew he didn't have the power to stop himself from sinning, so he held on to God. The fact that he didn't hold back the truth from God is what really set him apart.

Living authentically involves an honest confrontation with our true selves before God. It's recognising that God desires truthfulness and faithfulness from the depths of our hearts. Authenticity is cultivated in the secret chambers of our souls, where God imparts wisdom to those who seek it.

Psalm 51:6 serves as an invitation to delve into the core of our existence, to seek authenticity in the secret places of our hearts. It encourages us to embrace God's teaching and wisdom, allowing it to transform us into authentic beings who honour Him.

Let this verse be a catalyst in your journey towards authenticity. May it inspire you to seek truthfulness and wisdom in the deepest recesses of your being, fostering a life that authentically reflects God's desires.

Instead of looking at our sin and letting it envelop us with guilt and condemnation, Let's speak the truth to God.

Prayer:

Heavenly Father,

Grant me the courage to confront my true self before You. Teach me wisdom and truthfulness from the depths of my being. May authenticity resonate within me, shaping me into a vessel that honours You in every aspect of my life. In Jesus' name, amen.

Daily Reflection:

Embrace the transformative power of honest self-confrontation before God, seek wisdom, and live a life that truly honour God.

21
AUTHENTIC LOVE: THE HEART OF GENUINE LIVING

Scripture:

> *"Jesus replied: 'Love the Lord your God with all your heart and with all your soul and with all your mind.' This is the first and greatest commandment. And the second is like it: 'Love your neighbour as yourself.' All the Law and the Prophets hang on these two commandments"* **Matthew 22:37-40** (NIV).

Devotional

God's love for us is unconditional.

In the symphony of divine commands, authenticity finds its melody in the harmonious notes of love—love for God and love for others. Matthew 22:37-40 sums up the essence of authenticity in a life brimming with genuine love.

Love makes us go the extra mile, keeping us intentional and determined towards something or someone. If we say we love God, then we need to show it through our love for our fellow human beings, as they are the ones we can physically show that act of love. Our love for God is evident in the way we love others.

Some ways to show our love for God through our relationship with others include:

- Giving to the poor
- Praying for our people
- Feeding people
- Giving people that need a listening ear our time
- Spreading the good news to others

Love with no expectation from others; do it because God commanded it. That's the most important thing the world needs to be great, but many of us don't want to help others in any way. All we think about is me, myself and I.

If God sent Jesus to come to save only his close friends and family, do you think you'll be alive? Nope! Here is more reason why love should be part of our lifestyle.

Authentic living springs forth from a heart devoted to love. Jesus' response, when asked about the greatest commandment, underscores the centrality of love in authentic living. It's a call to wholeheartedly love God and extend that same love to our neighbours, echoing the foundational principles of a life rooted in authenticity.

Living authentically isn't a complex maze of rules and regulations but a simple yet profound call to love. It involves a genuine devotion to God that permeates every facet of our existence and overflows into compassionate love for those around us.

Matthew 22:37-40 serves as a roadmap for authentic living, reminding us that all aspects of life hinge on the foundation of love. It challenges us to authentically express our love for God and others, shaping our attitudes and actions.

Let this passage be a guiding light in your pursuit of authenticity. May it inspire you to love God wholeheartedly and extend genuine love to those around you, creating a life that authentically reflects God's love.

Prayer:

Gracious God, teach me to love You with all my heart, soul, and mind. Help me to extend genuine love to my neighbours as I love myself. May authenticity in love be the guiding principle of my life, shaping my actions and relationships. In Jesus' name, amen.

Daily Reflection:

God loves you unconditionally; living authentically is loving Him back wholeheartedly and extending genuine love to others.

22

AUTHENTIC REDEMPTION: THE FREEDOM OF GENUINE LIVING

Scripture:

> "*When you were dead in your sins and in the uncircumcision of your flesh, God made you alive with Christ. He forgave us all our sins, having cancelled the charge of our legal indebtedness, which stood against us and condemned us; he has taken it away, nailing it to the cross*" **Colossians 2:13-14** (NIV).

Devotional

We were all debtors under the bondage of sin, but God saw us in our sinful state and decided to save us from such evil so we can see the light(freedom).

In the depths of Colossians, authenticity shines through the transformative power of redemption. These verses unveil the heart of authentic living—a life liberated by the profound forgiveness and freedom found in Christ.

Authenticity blossoms from the soil of redemption. Paul's words remind us of our past state; we were dead in sin yet brought to life through Christ's redemptive work. This verse illuminates the authenticity of God's love—a love that forgives completely, cancelling our debts and setting us free from condemnation.

Living authentically is embracing the reality of our redemption in Christ. It's acknowledging our past and our imperfections and yet rejoicing in the truth that we have been made new. Authentic living involves walking in the freedom that Christ's sacrifice on the cross secured for us—freedom from guilt, shame, and condemnation.

We need the light of God to navigate life, which is why we need to accept God into our lives. He died for us so that we could wear a new garment of light.

Colossians 2:13-14 serves as a testament to the authenticity of God's grace—a grace that doesn't just cover but eradicates our sins, nailing them to the cross. It calls us to live authentically in this freedom, embracing the truth of our redemption daily.

Let this passage be a source of inspiration in your pursuit of authenticity. May it remind you of the completeness of Christ's redemptive work, empowering you to live authentically in the freedom and grace He has bestowed upon you.

Seize this opportunity of a new life that God has given to you to do exploits for God. Don't let it be a waste.

Prayer:

Heavenly Father,

Thank You for the authenticity of Your love and redemption in Christ. Help me live authentically in the freedom You have provided. Grant me the strength to embrace this redemption daily, walking in the assurance of Your forgiveness and grace. In Jesus' name, amen.

Daily Reflection:

It is the redemptive love of God that rescues you from the bondage of sin, inspiring authentic living rooted in the freedom and forgiveness that Christ gives.

23

AUTHENTICITY IN GOD'S EYES: THE HEART'S TRUE MEASURE

Scripture:

> *"But the Lord said to Samuel, 'Do not consider his appearance or his height, for I have rejected him. The Lord does not look at the things people look at. People look at the outward appearance, but the Lord looks at the heart'"* **1 Samuel 16:7** (NIV).

Devotional

Similar to judging a book by its cover, you might never know what's hidden inside if you don't search deeply. For human beings, we look at physical appearance, educational background, dress sense and many more, but God looks at the heart.

In the corridors of 1 Samuel, authenticity unfolds through the lens of God's perspective. This verse reveals a timeless truth—authenticity is found not in outward appearances but in the depths of the heart, where God's gaze rests.

Authentic living isn't about the external shell; it's about the condition of the heart. God's response to Samuel, seeking a new king, underscores the insignificance of outward appearances. It's a reminder that true authenticity is measured by the heart's alignment with God's will and character. If he had to choose by himself, he would have chosen one of David's brothers, and the fact that his father didn't consider him fit to be introduced to Samuel shows that the father had written him off based on his looks.

Living authentically involves a heart transformed by God's truth and grace. It's a call to pursue integrity, sincerity, and obedience to God's desires, knowing that He sees beyond the façade and peers into the depths of our intentions.

1 Samuel 16:7 serves as a guiding light in our pursuit of authenticity. It challenges us to shift our focus from external appearances to cultivating a heart that reflects God's values, attitudes, and desires—a heart laid bare before Him.

Let this passage be a catalyst for authenticity in your life. May it inspire you to nurture a heart that aligns with God's purposes, fostering a life that authentically honours Him in every aspect.

Prayer:

Heavenly Father,

Help me cultivate authenticity from the depths of my heart. Grant me the wisdom to seek alignment with Your will and values. May my thoughts, intentions, and actions reflect a heart that honours You above all. In Your loving gaze, may I find the true measure of authenticity. In Jesus' name, amen.

Daily Reflection:

God focuses on the heart rather than outward appearances, urging us to have a heart aligned with His will for genuine living.

24

EMBODYING GRACE AND FORGIVENESS TO LIVE AUTHENTICALLY

Scripture:

> *"Do not judge, and you will not be judged. Do not condemn, and you will not be condemned. Forgive, and you will be forgiven"* **Luke 6:37** (NIV).

Devotional

Grace is "*Unmerited Favour*".

God is so generous and compassionate as He gives us grace often.

In the tapestry of Luke's gospel, authenticity weaves itself through the fabric of forgiveness and grace. This verse reveals a profound truth—authenticity finds expression in a heart that extends grace and forgiveness, mirroring the nature of our gracious God.

Authentic living involves a disposition of grace and forgiveness. Jesus' words here unveil the authenticity found in refraining from judgement and condemnation. It's an invitation to reflect God's character, embodying a spirit of understanding and forgiveness towards others.

Living authentically isn't just about being true to oneself; it's about mirroring God's grace-filled nature. This verse challenges us to examine our attitudes, urging us to extend the same forgiveness and grace that we ourselves seek and receive from God.

We are still living under the grace of God, not because we deserve it but because God wants us to do the same for others and also make heaven. So let our words and actions towards people who err us or do evil to us be seasoned with grace. I mean, you can imagine someone praying for an armed robber who stole from them and even hurt them. It sounds ridiculous, right? But that's how God wants us to live.

Remember the two thieves that were placed beside Jesus during the crucifixion? They were guilty, but because one of them was bold enough to ask Jesus to take him with him if he was truly the son of God, he escaped eternal destruction. So who are we to judge if our God is this gracious?

Lessons from Luke 6:37 must guide us in our pursuit of authenticity. It inspires us to embrace a heart that forgives and refrains from judgement, fostering an environment of grace and authenticity in our relationships.

Let this verse be a catalyst for authentic living. May it inspire you to extend grace and forgiveness, cultivating authenticity in your interactions and reflecting God's unending grace and mercy.

Prayer:

Heavenly Father,

Grant me the grace to live authentically by extending forgiveness and grace to others. Help me refrain from judgement and condemnation, mirroring Your boundless love and forgiveness. May my actions reflect authenticity through the grace I extend to others. In Jesus' name, amen.

Daily Reflection:

Listen to the voice of Grace, calling out to you to authentically mirror God's compassion by extending forgiveness, compassion, and understanding to others.

25
AUTHENTIC LOVE: LIVING CONSCIENTIOUSLY

Scripture:

> *"Love must be sincere. Hate what is evil; cling to what is good"* **Romans 12:9** (NIV).

Devotional

God gave us the ability to know what is good and what is evil so we can monitor and correct ourselves when necessary.

In the tapestry of Romans, authenticity finds its essence in the sincerity of love. This verse encapsulates the core of authentic living—a life rooted in genuine and sincere love that abhors evil and clings fervently to goodness.

Our motive for loving people shouldn't be because of what we will gain from them or because we have a common enemy. It's important to love people just the way God loves us all, regardless of all our wrongs.

Just as the church should show love to one another and not hurt people or condemn them because of their sins or status, it's the home of Christ; therefore, there should be no fake love or hypocrisy.

The good Samaritan didn't think of personal gains when he helped the man armed robbers attacked; neither did he think it was none of his problems, and walked away from the scene. He showed love, ensuring that all the bills were paid. That's the love God wants us to exhibit in this cruel world without thinking too deeply about what we stand to benefit. God is the one who will reward us.

Authentic living begins with sincere love. Paul's exhortation to the Romans underscores the authenticity found in a love that is heartfelt and genuine. It's a call to cultivate a love that's not superficial but deeply rooted in truth and righteousness.

Living authentically isn't just about expressing love; it's about living out a love that discerns between good and evil. This verse challenges us to embrace goodness while vehemently rejecting evil, reflecting the authenticity of our love through our actions and choices.

Romans 12:9 serves as a guiding principle in our pursuit of authenticity. It urges us to love sincerely, allowing this authentic love to permeate every aspect of our lives, shaping our attitudes and actions.

Let this verse be a catalyst for authentic living. May it inspire you to cultivate a sincere love that discerns between good and evil, fostering authenticity in your relationships and reflecting God's love to those around you.

Prayer:

Heavenly Father,

Grant me the grace to love sincerely and authentically. Help me discern between good and evil, clinging passionately to what is good. May my love be genuine and heartfelt, reflecting Your love to those around me. In Jesus' name, amen.

Daily Reflection:

Every day of your life must be lived deliberately, doing good, and showing love, respect, and compassion to other. Remember, Christ loved you first.

26

INTEGRITY IN SPEECH: A PATH TO AUTHENTICITY

Scripture:

> *"Let your 'Yes' be 'Yes,' and your 'No,' 'No.' For whatever is more than these is from the evil one"* **Matthew 5:37** (NIV).

Devotional

Can people come to you and find your words true as you said them?

In the profound teachings of Jesus recorded in Matthew, authenticity resonates through the integrity of our words. This verse unveils a powerful truth—authenticity thrives in honest and straightforward communication, void of deceit or manipulation.

Authentic living involves sincerity in speech. Jesus' words here reveal the authenticity found in a commitment to truthfulness. It's an invitation to speak with integrity, ensuring that our words align with our actions, thereby reflecting the genuineness of our character.

Living authentically isn't merely about saying the right words; it's about being true to our promises and commitments. This verse challenges us to cultivate a spirit of honesty and reliability, fostering trustworthiness in our interactions with others.

No one wants an unreliable friend, boss, partner or person as a friend, someone that they can't boldly vouch for because everything they say is false or half-truth.

These days, there seems to be a rise in the number of deceitful, selfish and insincere people. We see that in relationships today, where ladies are deceived into relationships by men who promise to love them, only to find out that these men are already married but stay in different locations from their spouses. It's sad as a lady to experience that because you totally trusted that person, thinking you were both on the same page. It's sad to see the efforts people put into relationships while having bad intentions.

It breaks trust and makes others more cautious, and God is telling us today that he doesn't like that character, and anyone doing such has no love or truth in them.

Matthew 5:37 serves as a guiding principle in our pursuit of authenticity. It urges us to let our words be an honest reflection of our intentions, steering clear of falsehood or exaggeration that leads away from truthfulness.

Don't sell a product or service to someone when you know that it's not up to par; best believe that if your sweet words get them to buy it and they aren't satisfied with the quality, they will never work with you again.

To you, it's a gain in that moment, but it never lasts.

Let this verse be a catalyst for authentic living. May it inspire you to uphold integrity in your speech, cultivating a character marked by truthfulness and reliability, thus reflecting God's authenticity in your everyday interactions.

Prayer:

Heavenly Father,

Grant me the strength to speak with integrity and honesty. Help me uphold authenticity in my words, ensuring that my 'Yes' means 'Yes' and my 'No' means 'No.' May my speech reflect Your truthfulness and reliability. In Jesus' name, amen.

Daily Reflection:

Authentic living thrives in the integrity and honesty of your words. Today, you are admonished to align our speech with truthfulness.

27
AUTHENTIC TRANSPARENCY UNDER GOD'S WATCHFUL EYES

Scripture:

"*The eyes of the Lord are everywhere, keeping watch on the wicked and the good*" **Proverbs 15:3** (NIV).

Devotional

God sees it all.

There were times in the Bible when God's children suffered oppression and were held in captivity. In these times, they cried for help from their oppressors and wondered if God was aware. God says that even if a strand of your hair falls, He knows. That's how detailed God is.

In the timeless wisdom of Proverbs, authenticity shines through the lens of God's omnipresence. This verse unveils a profound truth—authenticity thrives in the knowledge that God sees our every action and motive, urging us towards genuine transparency.

Authentic living involves a recognition of God's constant presence. This verse reminds us that God's watchful eyes perceive both our righteousness and faults. It's an invitation to live authentically, knowing that we stand bare before the eyes of our Creator.

Now, when we know that God is always present, we begin to act in a conscious state. It's just like an examination where we have an invigilator. If you don't read for your exam and plan to cheat, you know you are going to be caught. That's how God watches over us as we take on the test of life.

God wants us to live our lives knowing fully well that he is there, and hopefully, we don't underestimate his omnipresence and sneak a few sins into our lives.

Living authentically isn't about hiding imperfections; it's about embracing vulnerability before God. This verse challenges us to be transparent, acknowledging our strengths and weaknesses and seeking God's guidance in every aspect of our lives.

Proverbs 15:3 serves as a reminder of God's unwavering gaze, encouraging us to live authentically in His presence. It calls us to be genuine and open-hearted, knowing that authenticity before God fosters intimacy and trust in our relationship with Him.

Let this verse be a catalyst for authentic living. May it inspire you to embrace transparency before God, allowing His presence to shape your character and actions, thus reflecting authenticity in your life.

Prayer:

Heavenly Father,

Help me to live authentically in Your presence. Grant me the courage to be transparent, acknowledging my strengths and weaknesses before You. May my authenticity foster a deeper relationship with You, knowing that Your watchful eyes guide and shape my life. In Jesus' name, amen.

Daily Reflection:

Nothing you do is hidden before God; He is present everywhere, seeing your actions and motives. Therefore, be inspired to live authentically with transparency before Him.

28

EMBRACING AUTHENTICITY THROUGH THE RENEWAL OF TRUE IDENTITY

Scripture:

> "*Do not lie to each other, since you have taken off your old self with its practices*" **Colossians 3:9** (NIV).

Devotional

Who are you in Christ?

There are some lies we tell that now seem very normal. An example is when a superior tells us to tell someone else that they are not around, knowing fully well that they are present. How do we go against a superior's command and still obey God's instruction?

There are better ways to address such cases; saying, " My boss is not free to take in visitors currently", sounds better than lying.

In the depth of Colossians, authenticity resonates through the call to discard falsehood and embrace truthfulness. This verse uncovers a profound truth—authenticity thrives in the abandonment of deceit, aligning with our renewed identity in Christ.

When you receive a new identity with Christ, you let go of pleasing men even though it will cost you something. Your salvation is more important.

Authentic living involves a departure from falsehood and pretence. Paul's instruction to the Colossians urges them to shed the old self, marked by deceitful practices, and embrace the truthfulness that comes with their new identity in Christ.

You can't change your old garment and still be lying, taking bribes, or imposing an honorarium as a means to preach or share the good news. Our lives need to look like what God wants and expects us to be. It shouldn't look like those of the world.

Living authentically isn't about perpetuating falsehood but aligning our actions and words with our renewed identity in Christ. This verse challenges us to embrace the truth that comes with being clothed in the character of Christ, fostering sincerity and honesty in our interactions.

Colossians 3:9 serves as a guiding light in our pursuit of authenticity. It calls us to discard the old habits of deceit and embrace the authenticity that comes with our new identity in Christ, shaping our character and relationships.

Let this verse be a catalyst for authentic living. May it inspire you to embrace truthfulness and honesty, aligning your life with the renewed identity found in Christ, thus reflecting authenticity in your thoughts, words, and actions.

Prayer:

Heavenly Father, help me to live authentically in alignment with my new identity in Christ. Grant me the strength to shed falsehood and embrace truthfulness. May my life reflect the authenticity found in my renewed identity, glorifying You in all I do. In Jesus' name, amen.

Daily Reflection:

Abandon deceit and embrace truthfulness, and reflect your renewed identity in Christ through authentic living.

29

GENUINE REFLECTIONS EMANATE FROM AN AUTHENTIC HEART

Scripture:

> *"Woe to you, teachers of the law and Pharisees, you hypocrites! You are like whitewashed tombs, which look beautiful on the outside but on the inside are full of the bones of the dead and everything unclean. In the same way, on the outside you appear to people as righteous but on the inside you are full of hypocrisy and wickedness"* **Matthew 23:27-28** (NIV).

Devotional

Have you ever seen a watermelon look so good outside only to cut it open and see that it's rotten? That's very sad and a total waste of money, cravings, and physical admiration.

In the poignant words of Jesus recorded in Matthew,

authenticity shines through the contrast between external appearances and internal reality. This passage uncovers a profound truth—authenticity resides not in outward displays but in the sincerity of the heart.

Authentic living involves more than surface appearances; it's about the genuine state of our hearts. Jesus' rebuke to the religious leaders illuminates the dichotomy between outward righteousness and inward hypocrisy. It challenges us to cultivate authenticity that springs from the depths of our character.

Reflection allows us to review our actions within a period and make adjustments where necessary. It's important to have those moments of just fixing what has to be fixed and realigning our lives with God.

Who would have thought that a disciple of God would be the one to betray him? But we see how Judas Iscariot sold Jesus to the chief priests for 30 silver coins. It shows that what is in a man's heart is more important than what they say to you or how they look. After Judas had sold Jesus, he felt guilty and returned the money, and instead of asking for forgiveness, he hung himself.

He followed Jesus, but I doubt his heart was ever truly with God, let alone understanding how God works.

Living authentically isn't about putting on a facade of righteousness; it's about genuine transformation within.

This verse calls us to align our inner selves with our outer expressions, fostering sincerity and genuine righteousness that stem from a heart transformed by God's grace.

Matthew 23:27-28 serves as a sobering reminder of the importance of inner authenticity. It urges us to examine our hearts, ensuring that our outward displays truly reflect the authenticity of our character and relationship with God.

Let this passage be a catalyst for authentic living. May it inspire you to seek inner authenticity, allowing God to transform your heart so your external expressions genuinely reflect the righteousness found in Him.

Prayer:

Heavenly Father,

Help me to cultivate authenticity from the depths of my heart. Grant me the grace to align my inner self with my outward expressions, reflecting sincerity and righteousness. May my life be a genuine reflection of Your transforming work within me. In Jesus' name, amen.

Daily Reflection:

Genuine authenticity comes from a sincere heart transformed by God's grace, not from mere outward appearances of righteousness. Is your heart transformed?

30

UNWAVERING ASSURANCE REFELECTED THROUGH THE AUTHENTICITY OF GOD'S LOVE

Scripture:

> "*For I am convinced that neither death nor life, neither angels nor demons, neither the present nor the future, nor any powers, neither height nor depth, nor anything else in all creation, will be able to separate us from the love of God that is in Christ Jesus our Lord*" **Romans 8:38-39** (NIV).

Devotional

Think of someone close to you that you trust telling you that they will get you something you asked for; no matter how long it takes them to, you will trust and wait on them to deliver it to you because they have earned your trust.

That's an assurance given due to past records. However, with God giving you life and certain things that you don't think you merit, why do you not take His words and promises over your life seriously?

Do you think God will forsake you after all He has done for you?

In the resounding promises of Romans, authenticity resonates through the unwavering nature of God's love. This verse unveils a profound truth—authenticity flourishes in the unshakable assurance of God's boundless and enduring love for us.

God has assured us to reign with Him if we serve Him (Romans 8:16-17). Remember the hymn *Blessed assurance, Jesus is mine?*

Authentic living is grounded in the certainty of God's love. Paul's words here echo a conviction that transcends any circumstance or challenge. It's an assurance that God's love remains constant, regardless of what we face in life.

Living authentically is embracing the unbreakable bond of God's love. This verse challenges us to anchor our identities and actions in the certainty of His love, fostering genuine confidence that nothing can separate us from His unwavering affection.

Romans 8:38-39 serves as an unyielding beacon of God's authentic love. It invites us to live fearlessly, knowing that His love transcends every boundary and circumstance, empowering us to live authentically in His grace.

Let this passage be a source of strength for authentic living. May it inspire you to embrace the certainty of God's love, allowing His unending affection to shape your identity and actions, thus reflecting authenticity in your faith journey.

Prayer:

Heavenly Father,

Thank You for the unshakable assurance of Your love. Grant me the grace to live authentically, rooted in the certainty of Your unwavering affection. May Your love empower me to face each day with confidence and authenticity in my faith. In Jesus' name, amen.

Daily Reflection:

God's love for you is steadfast and never-ceasing, so be encouraged to live authentically with the assurance that nothing can stop His love for you.

31

AUTHENTIC SERVICE: THE HEART OF WHOLEHEARTED EFFORT

Scripture:

> "*Whatever you do, work at it with all your heart, as working for the Lord, not for human masters, since you know that you will receive an inheritance from the Lord as a reward. It is the Lord Christ you are serving*" **Colossians 3:23-24** (NIV).

Devotional

In the profound exhortation of Colossians, authenticity resonates through the call to wholehearted service. This verse unveils a profound truth—authenticity thrives in the sincerity of our efforts, driven by a heart devoted to serving the Lord.

Authentic living involves wholehearted dedication in our endeavours. Paul's words here highlight the authenticity found in working diligently, not merely for human recognition but as an offering to the Lord. It's a call to infuse sincerity into every task, knowing that our service is ultimately unto God.

Living authentically isn't about surface-level efforts; it's about dedicating our work to God. This verse challenges us to approach our responsibilities with genuine commitment, understanding that our service, whether big or small, carries eternal significance when done for the Lord.

One of the most popular reasons why more people serve in God's vineyard is the popularity and appreciation that comes with it. Some ministers are eager to preach as guest ministers at other churches because of the gifts they receive. However, this is not true service to God–it's selfish.

This doesn't mean that people shouldn't be honoured, but what God wants from us is genuine service, one that doesn't ask for a reward after service from men but believes that God is a rewarder of good things and He will take care of them.

Let's use our skills to please God, and let's put in the effort we would have if we had been paid to do a job.

Colossians 3:23-24 serves as a guiding principle in our pursuit of authenticity. It urges us to work with sincerity and diligence, knowing that our authentic service to God brings an eternal reward.

Let this passage be a catalyst for authentic living. May it inspire you to approach your tasks with wholehearted dedication, knowing that in serving diligently, you honour God and reflect authenticity in your work and service.

Prayer:

Heavenly Father,

Help me work with sincerity and wholeheartedness, dedicating my efforts to You. Grant me the grace to serve diligently, knowing that my work is ultimately for Your glory. May my service reflect authenticity and honour You in all I do. In Jesus' name, amen.

Daily Reflections:

Re-evaluate your motives for doing the things you do. Remember that God seeks your wholehearted dedication, and your sincere efforts for Him will reflect true authenticity and bring you eternal reward.

32

INTEGRITY'S SHIELD: A PATH TO AUTHENTICITY

Scripture:

> "*Whoever walks in integrity walks securely, but whoever takes crooked paths will be found out*" **Proverbs 10:9** (NIV).

Devotional

If you solved a maths equation where you didn't really show the process or working but got the answer, you won't get a full mark for it like you would if you stated the process clearly and how you arrived at the answer. Demonstrating how you arrived at your answer shows more understanding and sincerity.

God is not only interested in what you do, but He is interested in why and how you did it. You can't get money through dubious means; send some to charity and expect God to applaud you. Men will because they don't know the source of your money or your motive, but God does.

In the wisdom-filled Proverbs, authenticity shines through the pathway of integrity. This verse uncovers a timeless truth—authenticity thrives in the unwavering commitment to walk with integrity, fostering security and trustworthiness.

Authentic living involves walking the path of integrity. The author's words underline the authenticity found in a life led by honesty and uprightness. It's an invitation to tread the path of integrity, knowing that it leads to a secure and trustworthy life.

Living authentically isn't about shortcuts or deceit; it's about navigating life with an unwavering commitment to honesty and truthfulness. This verse challenges us to embrace integrity as a shield, safeguarding our character and reputation. Proverbs 10:9 serves as a guiding principle in our pursuit of authenticity. It encourages us to uphold integrity, recognising that authenticity blossoms in the fertile ground of honest and upright living.

You can't bribe God; it's either you have integrity, or you don't, so stop using shortcuts and follow the path that God has laid for you. The man who uses dubious means to build a life and appears good in the eyes of men will soon be exposed, but those who live a sincere life will be praised.

Let this passage be a catalyst for authentic living. May it inspire you to walk securely in the path of integrity, fostering a life that reflects honesty and trustworthiness in all your dealings.

Prayer:

Heavenly Father, grant me the strength to walk in integrity and uprightness. Help me embrace honesty and truthfulness in all aspects of my life. May my actions and words reflect authenticity, grounded in the pathway of integrity. In Jesus' name, amen.

Daily Reflection:

Upholding integrity is a reflection of honesty, true security, and trustworthiness in all your actions.

33

AUTHENTIC REDEMPTION: THE CLEANSING POWER OF HONESTY

Scripture:

> *"Come now, let us settle the matter," says the Lord. "Though your sins are like scarlet, they shall be as white as snow; though they are red as crimson, they shall be like wool"* **Isaiah 1:18** (NIV).

Devotional

Redemption is the process of getting back something that was lost. In Christianity, we lost salvation due to sin, and for us to have access to God, we need to find our way back to God, which is where redemption comes in.

In the profound words of Isaiah, authenticity shines through the invitation to honesty and restoration. This verse unveils a transformative truth—authenticity thrives in the openness and sincerity of acknowledging our imperfections before God.

If you are currently serving God, you'll remember that a message had to get to you to remind you that you needed to fill a void in your life, and had to choose either to follow God or keep wallowing in sin.

Authentic living involves a transparent dialogue with God. The prophet's words echo an invitation to address our sinful state honestly. It's an invitation to embrace the cleansing power of God's forgiveness, transforming our scarlet sins into white-as-snow purity.

Living authentically isn't about hiding our flaws but bringing them openly to God for His cleansing touch. This verse challenges us to acknowledge our shortcomings, trusting in God's promise of forgiveness and restoration.

Isaiah 1:18 serves as a beacon of hope for authentic living. It urges us to come openly before God, knowing that our honesty leads to redemption and renewal—transforming our scarlet-stained lives into the purity of snow-white authenticity.

Let this passage be a catalyst for authentic living. May it inspire you to approach God with honesty, embracing His forgiveness and restoration, thus reflecting authenticity in your relationship with Him and others.

Prayer:

Heavenly Father,

Thank You for Your invitation to honesty and restoration. Help me come before You with authenticity, acknowledging my imperfections. May Your cleansing blood touch transform me, making my life a reflection of Your purity and grace. In Jesus' name, amen.

Daily Reflection:

Do you approach God with honesty or deceit? Lean on God's forgiveness and restoration, to transform your life into genuine honesty.

34
CRUCIFIED WITH CHRIST: AUTHENTICITY THROUGH SURRENDER

Scripture:

"I have been crucified with Christ and I no longer live, but Christ lives in me. The life I now live in the body, I live by faith in the Son of God, who loved me and gave himself for me" **Galatians 2:20** (NIV).

Devotional

Jesus said, "If anyone wishes to come after Me, he must deny himself, and take up his cross and follow Me" (Matthew 16:24). You must follow Jesus completely, withholding nothing from Him because He gave His life for us. So what is so important to you that is bigger than someone laying their life down for you? Nothing.

All God wants for us is to sacrifice our love for earthly desires and commit to serving Him, who has the better plan for our lives. The problem with surrendering is that we think we have the best plan and consider God as an option we have around that we give our Sundays to. Now, that limits our understanding of His Word and how powerful He is, making it difficult for us to submit to Him totally.

In the profound declaration of Paul in Galatians, authenticity resonates through the surrendered life to Christ. This verse uncovers a profound truth—authenticity thrives in complete surrender and identification with the life of Christ.

Authentic living involves surrendering our will to Christ. Paul's words echo a transformative reality of being crucified with Christ—letting go of our own desires and allowing Christ to live through us. It's an invitation to embrace Christ's life as our own. Living authentically isn't about self-promotion; it's about Christ's presence manifesting in our lives. This verse challenges us to surrender our ambitions, our goals, and our identity to Christ, allowing His life to shape and define ours.

Galatians 2:20 serves as a guiding principle in our pursuit of authenticity. It urges us to embrace the surrendered life, living by faith in Christ and allowing His love to motivate and guide our every action.

Let this passage be a catalyst for authentic living. May it

inspire you to surrender fully to Christ, allowing His life to be expressed through yours, thus reflecting authenticity in your faith and actions.

Prayer:

Heavenly Father,

Help me to surrender completely to You. May Your life be manifested in mine as I live by faith in Your Son, Jesus Christ. Guide my steps and let Your love motivate every aspect of my life. In surrender, may authenticity in Christ shine through me. In Jesus' name, amen.

Daily Reflection:

Surrender to Christ and watch Him express His life through yours, thereby reflecting authenticity in your faith and actions.

35
AUTHENTIC ACTION: THE GENUINE RESPONSE TO TRUTH

Scripture:

> *"Do not merely listen to the word, and so deceive yourselves. Do what it says. Anyone who listens to the word but does not do what it says is like someone who looks at his face in a mirror and, after looking at himself, goes away and immediately forgets what he looks like"* **James 1:22-24** (NIV).

Devotional

Have you ever seen someone get rich from prayers or listening to inspirational sermons alone?

Many times, we get so religious that it fuels our laziness because we expect God to come down and help us, which is wrong. Faith without works is dead!

God blesses what he sees in our hands, so we must take

necessary actions in every part of our lives. It also applies to habits, thoughts and people we plan to move towards or away from; we have to physically take action to start seeing results.

In the insightful words of James, authenticity emerges through actions inspired by truth. This passage uncovers a transformative truth—authenticity thrives in the genuine response to God's Word, translating into tangible actions.

Authentic living involves more than passive reception; it's about active obedience to God's truth. James' exhortation challenges us not to deceive ourselves by merely hearing God's Word but failing to put it into practice. It's an invitation to live out the truth we've received.

If Joseph had not interpreted the dreams of the butler in the prison, who would have recommended him to the pharaoh? And how would he have gained freedom from the prison? Our actions shouldn't only be based on what we will gain but how we can impact lives because by touching lives positively, we are paving the way to attract blessings for ourselves.

Living authentically isn't about empty gestures but the transformation that occurs when we embody God's Word. This passage challenges us to be like a person who, after seeing their reflection, remembers and acts upon what they have seen—applying God's truth to their lives.

James 1:22-24 serves as a guiding principle in our pursuit of authenticity. It encourages us to embrace God's Word actively. Therefore, let's allow this passage to be our catalyst for authentic living, allowing its truths to permeate our actions and character, thus reflecting authenticity in our obedience.

Prayer:

Heavenly Father,

Grant me the wisdom and strength to not just hear Your Word but to live it out. Help me to respond genuinely to Your truth, allowing it to shape my character and actions. May my life be a reflection of authentic obedience to Your Word. In Jesus' name, amen.

Daily Reflection;

Authentic living is beyond listening to God's Words but actively embodying it. Faith is the action that brings result!

36
AUTHENTIC DISCERNMENT AND WISDOM: THE HEART'S TRUE LONGINGS

Scripture:

> "*And this is my prayer: that your love may abound more and more in knowledge and depth of insight, so that you may be able to discern what is best and may be pure and blameless for the day of Christ*" **Philippians 1:9-10** (NIV).

Devotional

Authenticity shines through the pursuit of discernment guided by love and wisdom in Paul's heartfelt prayer to the Philippians. This passage unveils a transformative truth—authenticity thrives in a discerning heart shaped by love and insight.

Authentic living involves more than surface-level understanding; it's about discerning what truly matters. Paul's prayer underscores the authenticity found in abounding love combined with knowledge and depth of insight. It's an invitation to pursue discernment through the lens of love.

Living authentically isn't about external appearances; it's about purity and blamelessness from within. This passage challenges us to seek discernment, enabling us to distinguish what is best, aligning our lives with God's will and living blamelessly before Him.

Philippians 1:9-10 serves as a guiding prayer in our pursuit of authenticity. It encourages us to pray for a discerning heart shaped by love and wisdom, fostering authenticity in our choices and character.

When you are a child of God, you don't navigate life alone; you get special guidance on what to do, how to do it, and when and where to be. You don't do life with your common sense alone; instead, back it up with spiritual assistance.

To acquire the spirit of discernment, you need to:

- Spend more time with the word
- Understand the word/message
- Experience God's grace
- Begin to practise by waiting to hear from God
- Obey God's command

To encounter God, you need to put yourself in the right space to find him. Think of 'where' and 'how' you can find God. It's in your determination to know Him that you begin to embody the gifts of the spirit. When God sees your desire for Him, He will carry you up like a baby, stretching his hands for his mother to pick him up, and He'll guide you through His Word.

Let this passage be a catalyst for authentic living. May it inspire you to seek discernment guided by love and wisdom, allowing God's truth to shape your character and actions, thus reflecting authenticity in your life.

Prayer:

Heavenly Father,

Grant me a discerning heart filled with love and wisdom. Help me to seek what truly matters, aligning my life with Your will. May I grow in authenticity, living blamelessly before You and others. In Jesus' name, amen.

Daily Reflection:

On the journey to authentic living, ensure you discern and focus on what truly matters and maintain deep relationship with God.

37

AUTHENTIC TRANSFORMATION: RENEWAL THROUGH THE KNOWLEDGE OF CHRIST

Scripture:

> *"Do not lie to each other, since you have taken off your old self with its practices and have put on the new self, which is being renewed in knowledge in the image of its Creator"* **Colossians 3:9-10** (NIV).

Devotional

If you keep wearing rag clothes, it will be difficult to identify yourself with sane and wealthy people.

You have to look the part to play the path right because while men look at the physical appearance, God looks at the heart. When you tell people that you encountered a rich man, they expect changes in your life, similar to having an encounter with God. There needs to be a transformation to validate the change.

In the insightful words of Paul to the Colossians, authenticity emerges through the transformative process of putting off the old self and embracing the new. This passage unveils a profound truth—authenticity thrives in the ongoing renewal and alignment with God's image. That is, shedding the falsehood of the old self and embracing the authenticity of the new. Paul's instruction challenges us not to deceive one another but to live genuinely, reflecting the transformation initiated by Christ.

Living authentically isn't about maintaining pretence but about embracing continual renewal. This passage urges us to clothe ourselves with the new self, marked by a constant renewal in the knowledge of our Creator and lives aligned with His image.

Colossians 3:9-10 serves as a guiding principle in our pursuit of authenticity. It encourages us to live in the reality of our transformed selves, renewed daily to reflect the image of God.

When you say you are a child of God, it has to show in your speech, dress, reasoning, relationships and circle of friends. Don't expect people to believe the gospel you are trying to preach, looking or acting like a child of the world.

Let this passage be a catalyst for authentic living. May it inspire you to embrace the continual renewal offered through Christ, aligning your life with His image and reflecting authenticity in your character and actions.

Prayer:

Heavenly Father,

Thank You for the ongoing renewal You offer through Christ. Help me to live authentically, shedding the falsehood of my old self and embracing the authenticity of the new. May my life reflect Your image as I am continually renewed in Your knowledge. In Jesus' name, amen.

Daily Reflection

To truly live in authenticity, you have to shed your old self (let go of the past) and embrace continual renewal.

38
UPHOLDING INTEGRITY IN SPOKEN WORDS: THE POWER OF AUTHENTICITY

Scripture:

"Above all, my brothers and sisters, do not swear—not by heaven or by earth or by anything else. All you need to say is a simple 'Yes' or 'No.' Otherwise you will be condemned" **James 5:12** (NIV).

Devotional

In the concise yet powerful words of James, authenticity resonates through the integrity of our speech. This verse uncovers a profound truth—authenticity thrives in honest, straightforward communication devoid of oaths or unnecessary embellishments.

Authentic living involves a commitment to truthful speech. James urges us to let our 'Yes' be 'Yes' and our 'No' be 'No.' It's an invitation to uphold integrity in our words, ensuring that our speech reflects the genuineness of our character.

Owning up to our mistakes or even saying what we are sure of can be hard because there is always a word "But" that gives a reason for why we did it, But God right here is telling us to let go of the "BUT" and say the truth as it is.

Think about Adam and Eve when they ate the apple, and their eyes opened. They didn't want to say the truth without justifying their actions. “Why did you eat the apple, Eve?” If Eve had said, “I ate it because I desired it, and I was wrong”. This response would have sounded better than "The devil lured me?"

No need to summon the dead to make people know that what you are saying is true. If you did it, say, “Yes, I did this”. If they ask for further explanations, then you can make it known.

Living authentically isn't about making extravagant promises or using elaborate language; it's about simplicity and truthfulness. This verse challenges us to speak honestly and directly, letting our words carry the weight of our character.

James 5:12 serves as a guiding principle in our pursuit of authenticity. It encourages us to uphold integrity in our speech, fostering trustworthiness and authenticity in our interactions with others.

Let this passage be a catalyst for authentic living. May it inspire you to speak with honesty and integrity, ensuring that your words reflect the authenticity and sincerity of your character.

Prayer:

Heavenly Father, grant me the grace to speak truthfully and with integrity. Help me to uphold authenticity in my speech, ensuring that my words align with the genuineness of my character. May my 'Yes' be 'Yes' and my 'No' be 'No,' reflecting Your truth in all I say. In Jesus' name, amen.

Daily Reflection:

Does your 'Yes' means 'Yes' and 'No' means 'No'? Let your words reflect the integrity of your character because authentic living established in truthful words.

39
EMBRACING FORGIVENESS: THE HEART OF AUTHENTICITY

Scripture:

> *"Bear with each other and forgive one another if any of you has a grievance against someone. Forgive as the Lord forgave you"* **Colossians 3:13** (NIV).

Devotional

There are some people we find so annoying and some others who have repeatedly done some hurtful things that make us start resenting them. Then we find ourselves constantly referencing those incidents, forming a negative perception of those people. However, the truth is that no one is perfect, and until we understand this, we will continue to think everyone has a problem.

Forgive!

The moment we start defining people by their wrongdoings towards us, it's difficult to see them in a good light, and that makes us hate them. Hate is a sin.

In Paul's compassionate guidance to the Colossians, authenticity shines through the act of forgiveness. This verse reveals a profound truth—authenticity thrives in the willingness to forgive, mirroring the grace we've received from the Lord.

Authentic living involves the extension of forgiveness. Paul's exhortation challenges us not to hold grievances against one another but to forgive, just as the Lord forgave us. It's an invitation to embody the grace and compassion we've experienced.

Therefore, let us not harbour resentment; rather, we release grudges and extend the same forgiveness we've received, allowing love and reconciliation to flourish.

Colossians 3:13 serves as a guiding principle in our pursuit of authenticity. It encourages us to embrace forgiveness, fostering genuine relationships marked by grace and reconciliation.

Let this verse be a catalyst for authentic living. May it inspire you to extend forgiveness as you've been forgiven, fostering authentic relationships and reflecting the grace of God in your interactions.

Prayer:

Heavenly Father,

Grant me the strength to forgive as You've forgiven me. Help me release any grievances and extend grace and compassion to others. May my actions reflect Your forgiveness and foster authenticity in my relationships. In Jesus' name, amen.

Daily Reflection:

Free your heart from harbouring resentment, anger, and grudges. Let forgiveness, love and reconciliation lead.

40

WALKING IN TRUTH: THE PATH TO AUTHENTICITY

Scripture:

> *"Therefore each of you must put off falsehood and speak truthfully to your neighbour, for we are all members of one body"* **Ephesians 4:25** (NIV).

Devotional

God wants us to be hearers and doers of his word. Always!

In the profound counsel of Paul to the Ephesians, authenticity emerges through the commitment to truthfulness in speech. This verse uncovers a transformative truth—authenticity thrives in honest and transparent communication, fostering unity among believers.

Authentic living involves shedding falsehood and embracing truthfulness. Paul's instruction challenges us to speak truthfully to one another, recognizing our interconnectedness as members of the same body of believers.

Living authentically isn't about deception or pretence; it's about embracing transparency and sincerity. This verse urges us to communicate honestly, fostering trust and unity within the community of believers.

Ephesians 4:25 serves as a guiding principle in our pursuit of authenticity. It encourages us to speak truthfully, fostering genuine relationships and reflecting the authenticity of Christ in our interactions. No matter the reason you want to give for being dishonest, it is bad, which shows it's possible to be an honest person. God also wants to work with honest people who won't try to make money off the spiritual gifts He has given to them.

Gehazi was not an honest man who worked for Prophet Elisha, but one day, he showed his true character and earned himself and his generation a curse. He went to Naaman to collect gifts that had been rejected by prophet Elisha and lied that his boss had asked for them. Elisha, being a man filled with the spirit, saw this and asked him if he did it, and he denied it. Elisha immediately cursed him to have the leprosy that Naaman was delivered of.

I don't think any of us want to lose our health, life or salvation because of lies, so let's do better like Joseph, who was an honest servant. Be Honest.

People love to mingle with honest people because they are straightforward and can be entrusted with big tasks. People easily vouch for honest people because of their track record.

Let this verse be a catalyst for authentic living. May it inspire you to communicate with honesty and transparency, fostering unity and trust among believers and reflecting the authenticity of Christ in your speech.

Prayer:

Heavenly Father,

Grant me the grace to speak truthfully and transparently. Help me to put off falsehood and embrace honesty in my interactions with others. May my words reflect the authenticity of Christ, fostering unity and trust within the community of believers. In Jesus' name, amen.

Daily Reflection:

Authentic living means carrying God's truth wherever we go, showing truthfulness in our interaction with others, and promoting peace and unity among others.

41

FRUIT OF AUTHENTICITY: THE SPIRIT'S WORK WITHIN

Scripture:

> "*But the fruit of the Spirit is love, joy, peace, forbearance, kindness, goodness, faithfulness, gentleness and self-control. Against such things there is no law*" **Galatians 5:22-23** (NIV).

Devotional

In the rich tapestry of Paul's words to the Galatians, authenticity blossoms through the fruit of the Spirit. This verse unveils a transformative truth—authenticity thrives in the display of Christ-like virtues produced by the Spirit within.

Authentic living involves bearing the fruit of the Spirit. Paul's description paints a vivid picture of the characteristics that flow from a life surrendered to the Holy Spirit. We are admonished to allow these virtues to shape our attitudes and actions.

Living authentically isn't about striving through our own strength; it's about yielding to the Spirit's work within us. These verses challenge us to manifest the qualities of love, joy, peace, patience, kindness, goodness, faithfulness, gentleness, and self-control in our daily lives.

If it wasn't possible, God wouldn't give these rules to us and to attain that height of manifesting, all we need to do is seek God and intentionally act in accordance with His Word.

It's just like learning to be more organised when performing tasks without leaving any tasks unattended. We start by creating a list of our tasks and breaking them down into daily to-do lists with a time frame attached to each one. That way, it keeps you accountable to the point where it becomes part of you. You don't exhibit all these characteristics by keeping them in your head, but by putting them into practice every day, and when we fail today, we go again tomorrow stronger till we master it.

Galatians 5:22-23 serves as a guiding principle in our pursuit of authenticity. It encourages us to yield to the Spirit's work, allowing His fruit to be evident in our character, thus reflecting the authenticity of Christ within us.

God also sent us the Holy Spirit to always assist us in our journey to living a life that embodies these fruits of the Spirit because we can't do it alone, so open your heart and ears and listen attentively to the voice or promptings of the Holy Spirit.

Let this passage be a catalyst for authentic living. May it inspire you to yield to the Spirit's work, allowing His fruit to blossom in your life, thus reflecting the authenticity of Christ's character in all you do.

Prayer:

Heavenly Father,

Thank You for the work of Your Spirit within me. Help me yield to His leading and bear the fruit of love, joy, peace, and all the virtues described. May my life be a reflection of the authenticity found in Christ through the work of Your Spirit within me. In Jesus' name, amen.

Daily Reflection:

You live authentically when you submit to the Holy Spirit, allow His virtues to shape your character, and reflect Christ's authenticity in your daily affairs.

42

TRUE WORSHIP: THE HEART OF AUTHENTICITY

Scripture:

> "*God is spirit, and his worshippers must worship in the Spirit and in truth*" **John 4:24** (NIV).

Devotional

In the profound words of Jesus to the Samaritan woman, authenticity shines through the essence of true worship. This verse reveals a transformative truth—authenticity thrives in worship that emanates from the heart and aligns with truth.

One of the things we forget is that God is not a man, and the only way we can thank Him is through praise and worship. Singing praises to Him with a sincere and clean heart moves Him to do more and turn His face to us.

God also looks at the heart, not the dance steps or voice. It's easy to mistake dramatic acts for worship because they look so raw and pleasing to the eyes, but God knows those who are His and those who are acting righteous in His eyes. So make sure you are worshipping for the right reasons and with an open heart.

Authentic living involves genuine worship from the heart. Jesus' statement underscores the authenticity found in worshipping God in spirit and truth rather than mere external rituals. It's an invitation to engage with God sincerely and genuinely.

Living authentically isn't about outward displays; it's about heartfelt worship that aligns with God's truth. This verse challenges us to approach worship not just with words and actions but with a heart surrendered to God's Spirit and grounded in His truth.

Worshipping God shouldn't be based on when we are happy alone; we should also praise God when we aren't so happy because God will still come through for us.

John 4:24 serves as a guiding principle in our pursuit of authenticity. It urges us to worship God from the depths of our being, embracing sincerity and truthfulness in our connection with Him.

Let this verse be a catalyst for authentic living. May it inspire you to worship from the depths of your heart, embracing truth and sincerity in your relationship with God, reflecting the authenticity of your worship.

Prayer:

Heavenly Father,

Help me to worship You in spirit and truth. May my worship be authentic, arising from the depths of my heart and aligning with Your truth. Guide me in genuine worship that reflects the sincerity of my relationship with You. In Jesus' name, amen.

Daily Reflection:

Your praise and worship to God are the food He eats; do not starve Him of them. Actually, praising Him is in your own interest because if you don't, the stones can.

43

EMBRACING AUTHENTIC REPENTANCE: THE PATH TO RESTORATION

Scripture:

> "*Whoever conceals their sins does not prosper, but the one who confesses and renounces them finds mercy*" **Proverbs 28:13** (NIV).

Devotional

In the wisdom-filled words of Proverbs, authenticity emerges through the pathway of genuine repentance. This verse uncovers a transformative truth—authenticity thrives in the sincerity of confessing and turning away from wrongdoing, leading to mercy and restoration.

Authentic living involves honest repentance and confession. This verse challenges us not to conceal our faults but to embrace transparency before God. It's an invitation to acknowledge our shortcomings and seek forgiveness with a genuine desire to change.

Sometimes, we try to look holy and perfect because we don't want others to condemn us, and so instead of paying attention to how God sees us, we focus on how we think we should look to the world, which takes away the true meaning of living authentically.

True service to God is not an "Act" but a continuous process of learning, unlearning and growing.

Living authentically isn't about hiding mistakes; it's about acknowledging them and seeking restoration. This verse urges us to confess our sins and turn away from them, knowing that true authenticity is found in the path of repentance and mercy.

Proverbs 28:13 serves as a guiding principle in our pursuit of authenticity. It encourages us to embrace sincere repentance, finding mercy and restoration through genuine confession and a heart turned towards change.

Despite denying Jesus three times, Peter felt remorse and still ran back to Him when He resurrected. Remember that Jesus foresaw it and told Peter, who said he would not deny Jesus. He was so sure he wouldn't and was probably banking on his wisdom and love for following Jesus everywhere. However, Jesus was just trying to show him how human he could be, not to condemn him, but to draw him closer and make him understand that even when he makes those mistakes, he should not condemn himself but should run to God for forgiveness.

We find our strength in God; if we could do life by ourselves, we won't lean on God.

Let this verse be a catalyst for authentic living. May it inspire you to approach God with honesty, confess your faults, and seek His mercy and restoration, thus reflecting the authenticity of your repentance.

Prayer:

Heavenly Father,

Grant me the courage to confess my faults and turn away from wrongdoing. Help me to embrace authentic repentance and seek Your mercy and restoration. May my heart be sincere in seeking Your forgiveness and grace. In Jesus' name, amen.

Daily Reflection:

Embrace your authenticity before God and seek genuine transformation and restoration. God isn't seeking a perfect soul. Rather, He wants obedient and imperfect beings that desire Him.

44

AUTHENTIC STEWARDSHIP: THE GRACE OF SERVING

Scripture:

"Each of you should use whatever gift you have received to serve others, as faithful stewards of God's grace in its various forms. If anyone speaks, they should do so as one who speaks the very words of God. If anyone serves, they should do so with the strength God provides, so that in all things God may be praised through Jesus Christ. To him be the glory and the power forever and ever. Amen" **1 Peter 4:10-11** (NIV).

Devotional

No one is born without a gift, but many people haven't identified their gift, while some are clueless about how to use it to serve God. These gifts could be singing, writing, teaching, painting, dancing and many more. In a world where money is a high determinant of success and good living, we might use these gifts to make money only and not to the glory of God.

Don't get me wrong, money is good too, but when the only purpose of showcasing our gifts is to make money, then we might deviate from the path that God has set for us.

In the profound counsel of Peter, authenticity blossoms through the gracious use of our gifts for the service of others. This passage unveils a transformative truth—authenticity thrives in stewarding God's grace, reflecting His character through our actions and words.

Authentic living involves using our gifts to serve others. Peter encourages us to be faithful stewards of God's diverse grace, whether in speaking or serving. It's an invitation to employ our gifts in ways that honour God, reflecting His love and truth.

Living authentically isn't about self-promotion; it's about showcasing God's grace through our actions and speech. This passage urges us to serve and speak in ways that glorify God, recognising that it's His strength that empowers us.

1 Peter 4:10-11 serves as a guiding principle in our pursuit of authenticity. It encourages us to steward God's grace faithfully, reflecting His love, truth, and power in our service to others.

Let this passage be a catalyst for authentic living. May it inspire you to utilise your gifts graciously, serving and speaking in ways that glorify God, reflecting the authenticity of His grace in your life.

Prayer:

Heavenly Father,

Thank You for the gifts and grace You've bestowed upon me. Grant me the wisdom to steward them faithfully in service to others. May my words and actions reflect Your love and truth, glorifying You in all I do. Empower me with Your strength as I serve others for Your glory. In Jesus' name, amen.

Daily Reflection:

Build on impact before thinking of the money you'll make from the gift God has given you.

45

FORGIVENESS AS A WEAPON FOR AUTHENTIC LIVING

Scripture:

> *"For if you forgive other people when they sin against you, your heavenly Father will also forgive you. But if you do not forgive others their sins, your Father will not forgive your sins"* **Matthew 6:14-15** (NIV).

Devotional

Have you ever tried to forgive someone when you are still hurting from the pains they caused you? Or someone who you think doesn't deserve it?

I'm sure it's one of the most annoying feelings ever, but you still have to forgive regardless. Unforgiveness grows into bitterness, and just like that, we don't think good of anyone. We prefer to pay evil for evil and still dwell in God's presence.

How do we expect to create a room for God to dwell in us when we harbour so much bitterness? Take out that load and let God take charge.

In the compassionate teachings of Jesus, authenticity emerges through the willingness to forgive others. This verse unveils a transformative truth—authenticity thrives in the grace of forgiving others, mirroring the forgiveness we've received from God.

Authentic living involves embracing forgiveness. Jesus' words challenge us to extend forgiveness to others, knowing that our forgiveness from God is interconnected with our willingness to forgive others.

Living authentically isn't about holding onto grudges; it's about extending grace and mercy. This verse urges us to release bitterness and extend forgiveness, reflecting the authenticity of our relationship with God in our relationships with others.

Remember the servant who owed his boss some money and was about to be put in jail, but then he begged and was forgiven and told to go home? On his way back, he met someone who owed him, and immediately, he beat the man and threw him in jail. His boss heard the news and was displeased at how his ex-servant couldn't extend the same grace and forgiveness he received to the other debtor, so he ordered for him and threw him in prison.

Matthew 6:14-15 serves as a guiding principle in our pursuit of authenticity. It encourages us to forgive others, understanding that forgiveness is central to our relationship with God and to our authenticity as His followers.

God wants us to give grace to others and be compassionate just like he does to us.

Let this verse be a catalyst for authentic living. May it inspire you to extend forgiveness, releasing resentment and bitterness, thus reflecting the authenticity of God's grace in your relationships.

Prayer:

Heavenly Father,

Grant me the strength and grace to forgive others as You've forgiven me. Help me release any bitterness or resentment and extend grace and forgiveness to those who have wronged me. May my actions reflect the authenticity of Your forgiveness and grace in my life. In Jesus' name, amen.

Daily Reflection:

Forgiving yourself and others allow you free your mind from hurts and pains, thereby creating newness, freshness, new beginnings and an opportunity to emerge authentically.

46

EMBRACING TRUE WORTH: THE PURSUIT OF AUTHENTICITY

Scripture:

> "*But whatever were gains to me I now consider loss for the sake of Christ. What is more, I consider everything a loss because of the surpassing worth of knowing Christ Jesus my Lord, for whose sake I have lost all things. I consider them garbage, that I may gain Christ and be found in him, not having a righteousness of my own that comes from the law, but that which is through faith in Christ—the righteousness that comes from God on the basis of faith*" **Philippians 3:7-9** (NIV).

Devotional

In Paul's profound reflections, authenticity emerges through prioritising knowing Christ above all else. This passage uncovers a transformative truth—authenticity thrives in valuing the relationship with Christ above worldly gains or achievements.

Dying to oneself and forsaking whatever worldly possession or desire that will shift our focus from God is one of the ways to embrace authenticity. The fact that we are in pursuit of authenticity doesn't take away the fact that we are imperfect, but it shows our determination to live for God, which is the most important thing God looks out for. *A heart that is longing to see and live for God's approval.*

Authentic living involves reassessing our priorities. Paul's testimony challenges us to consider everything else as insignificant compared to the immeasurable worth of knowing Christ intimately.

Living authentically isn't about self-righteousness or worldly accomplishments; it's about finding our identity and worth in Christ alone. This passage urges us to seek righteousness through faith in Christ rather than relying on our own efforts or accolades.

Philippians 3:7-9 serves as a guiding principle in our pursuit of authenticity. It encourages us to treasure the knowledge of Christ above all, finding our true worth in Him rather than in worldly measures of success. When we find our worth in God, we escape the cage of condemnation, but when we seek validation from men, we lose our true essence.

The goal is to serve a God that we can't see but trust.

Let this passage be a catalyst for authentic living, inspiring you to reevaluate your priorities, placing the knowledge of Christ above all, and finding your true identity and worth in Him.

Prayer:

Heavenly Father,

Help me to value the knowledge of Christ above all worldly gains. Guide me in prioritising my relationship with Jesus, finding my worth and identity in Him alone. May I embrace authenticity by seeking righteousness through faith in Christ alone. In His precious name, amen.

Daily Reflection:

At the end of our sojourn on earth, our hustling and bustling, quest for worldly gains and material accumulations wouldn't matter anymore; only your gain in Christ will. Pursue authenticity with the awareness that Christ is the ultimate gain.

47

EMBRACING COMPASSIONATE FORGIVENESS: THE HEART OF AUTHENTICITY

Scripture:

> "*Be kind and compassionate to one another, forgiving each other, just as in Christ God forgave you*" **Ephesians 4:32** (NIV).

Devotional

In the compassionate exhortation of Paul to the Ephesians, authenticity emerges through the practice of forgiveness and compassion. This verse uncovers a transformative truth—authenticity thrives in the gracious extension of forgiveness, mirroring the forgiveness we've received from God.

Authentic living involves displaying kindness and compassion. Paul's words challenge us not only to forgive but also to embody kindness and compassion towards one another, reflecting the heart of Christ's forgiveness towards us.

Living authentically isn't about holding onto grudges but extending grace and understanding. This verse urges us to cultivate a spirit of forgiveness and compassion, reflecting the authenticity of God's love and mercy in our relationships.

Remember that the harlot that was brought to Jesus for judgement found mercy and forgiveness. If anything, He should have condemned her to death, but God doesn't hate His children, so He is always waiting for us to come back to Him as the prodigal son did.

In the normal sense, we want people to pay for the hurt they caused us, but God is reminding us to be like Jesus and not fault any man. Rather, we should pray for them.

Ephesians 4:32 serves as a guiding principle in our pursuit of authenticity. It encourages us to forgive and show compassion, understanding that forgiveness is central to reflecting the character of Christ.

Let this verse be a catalyst for authentic living. May it inspire you to extend forgiveness, kindness, and compassion to others, thus reflecting the authenticity of God's grace in your relationships.

Prayer:

Heavenly Father,

Grant me the grace to forgive others as You've forgiven me. Help me to extend kindness and compassion, mirroring Your love and mercy in my interactions with others. May my actions reflect the authenticity of Your forgiveness and grace in my life. In Jesus' name

Daily Reflection:

Just as you have been forgiven by God, extend compassionate forgiveness to others. Let your heart be free from holding anything unclean against any man. Forgive!

48

UPHOLDING HONESTY: THE PATH OF AUTHENTICITY

Scripture:

> "*The Lord detests lying lips, but he delights in people who are trustworthy*" **Proverbs 12:22** (NIV).

Devotional

In the wisdom-filled verses of Proverbs, authenticity shines through the virtue of honesty. This passage reveals a transformative truth—authenticity thrives in the integrity and trustworthiness of our words and actions.

Authentic living involves embracing honesty and trustworthiness. Proverbs highlight the disdain for deceitful speech while emphasising the delight found in those who uphold truth and reliability.

Living authentically isn't about deception or pretence but honesty and integrity in our interactions. This verse urges us to speak truthfully and act reliably, reflecting the authenticity of our character and our relationship with God.

Honesty should be something we portray every day of our lives, not just in certain situations. In Christ, there is no big, white, or small lie. Let's not be deceived by society's definition of honesty. It seems impossible when we want to stay out of people's way, so we agree to sign papers with inflated figures or say we saw what we didn't. Those are all lies and can't be justified in the sight of God.

Don't let Satan give you reasons why some lies are justified. Abraham almost lost his wife, Mary, because he lied that she was his sister out of fear, but God wasn't happy with him and spoke to the king through a dream not to do anything with Mary because she was married. God's mercy saved Abraham; don't make the same mistake because you are scared to speak the truth boldly.

Proverbs 12:22 serves as a guiding principle in our pursuit of authenticity. It encourages us to uphold honesty and reliability, understanding that these qualities align with God's desires for our character.

Let this verse be a catalyst for authentic living. May it inspire you to speak truthfully, act reliably, and uphold honesty in all aspects of your life, reflecting the authenticity of your character and your commitment to God.

Prayer:

Heavenly Father,

Help me to be a person of honesty and trustworthiness. Grant me the strength to speak truthfully and act with integrity in all situations. May my words and actions reflect the authenticity of Your character and bring glory to Your name. In Jesus' name, amen.

Daily Reflection:

There is no excuse for lying; no 'white lie', 'good lie' or 'half-truth' is justifiable. With boldness, integrity, and honesty, speak the truth and stand for what's right always.

49
AUTHENTIC FAITH AND THE HEART OF CONVICTION

Scripture:

"But in your hearts revere Christ as Lord. Always be prepared to give an answer to everyone who asks you to give the reason for the hope that you have. But do this with gentleness and respect, keeping a clear conscience, so that those who speak maliciously against your good behavior in Christ may be ashamed of their slander" **1 Peter 3:15-16** (NIV).

Devotional

In the profound words of Peter, authenticity emerges through a deep reverence for Christ and a genuine expression of faith. This passage uncovers a transformative truth—authenticity thrives in the sincere articulation of our hope in Christ, coupled with a spirit of gentleness and respect.

There will be days when our faith in God will get people angry and confused because they don't understand how we can trust in a person that we don't see. That shouldn't rile us up or make us shame them for their unbelief; rather, we should explain to them why we have so much faith and hope in God in a respectful way. By that, we could make them want to be saved, too.

During Jesus' earthly ministry, many people questioned His identity, but instead of being mean, He used parables and simple words to explain who He was, and He did it confidently.

Authentic living involves expressing our faith with gentleness and respect. Peter encourages believers to be prepared to share their faith, yet with humility and a clear conscience, so that our actions align with our words, showcasing the authenticity of our convictions.

Living authentically isn't about forceful arguments; it's about expressing our faith graciously. This verse urges us to respond to questions about our faith with gentleness and respect, allowing our conduct and words to bear witness to the authenticity of our beliefs.

1 Peter 3:15-16 serves as a guiding principle in our pursuit of authenticity. It encourages us to articulate our faith with humility, kindness, and a clear conscience, thereby reflecting the authenticity of Christ in our lives.

Let this passage be a catalyst for authentic living. May it inspire you to express your faith graciously, with gentleness and respect, thereby demonstrating the authenticity of your convictions in Christ.

Prayer:

Heavenly Father,

Grant me the wisdom and grace to share my faith authentically. Help me to express my beliefs with gentleness and respect, allowing my actions and words to reflect the sincerity of my convictions in Christ. May Your light shine through me as I live out an authentic faith. In Jesus' name, amen.

Daily Reflection:

What will you do when your faith is questioned? How will you react when your faith is tested? Will you stand firm, holding on to your conviction and belief in Christ? Will you gracefully answer questions about your identity in Christ? Or just get angry and evade questions?

Remember, your reaction or response can touch souls and bring them to Christ.

50
APPRECIATION AND GRATITUDE FOR THE GIFT OF AUTHENTICITY

Scripture:

> "*A jubilee shall that fiftieth year be to you; in it you shall neither sow, nor reap what grows of itself, nor gather the grapes from the undressed vines. For it is a jubilee; it shall be holy to you; you shall eat what it yields out of the field*" **Leviticus 25:11-12** (KJV).

Devotional

Our purpose on earth is not to acquire riches and make a name; God brought us here to reference Him in everything we do. When we look back at our journey in life, we want to smile and be grateful for the lessons we have learnt over the years. We look forward to more growth and walking with God in our journey in life.

Jesus lived an authentic life. If we trace down His earthly

ministry and look at how much He lived for God and withstood the persecution and hate from people just because He proved to be different, we understand that our life is for God and should be lived for Him only. He didn't focus on the hate; rather, He paid attention to the goal of touching lives, winning souls for God, and teaching others how to live for GOD. In all these, He still cared for the people who hurt Him, so much so that He died on the cross of Calvary for the sins that He didn't commit.

That's the Best biblical example of authenticity, dying to this world and living for God alone.

He lived for God's will to be made manifest.

Are you willing to let God walk you through this journey?

Whenever we feel like life has been so difficult and living for God is hard, let's reflect on the journey of how we started and where we are now. Good things require sacrifice, which is letting go of comfort and societal acceptance.

We have the likes of Abraham, Joseph, Moses, David, Esther, Jesus, Job and many more in the bible who took God along with them on their journey and humbled themselves through it all. You can do the same, too.

Living a Christ-like life is what authenticity is all about, and taking action right now is the first step to living that life.

Prayer:

Lord, I believe that you have brought me to this world with a purpose; please don't let me live a basic life. Make me the authentic being you want me to be, and give me the strength and desire to always look up to you as I take on this journey to Authenticity with you. Amen

Daily Reflection:

Show gratitude for how you started your authenticity journey, show gratitude for where you are at, and show gratitude for where Christ is leading you on your authenticity journey.

It might not look like it yet, but with God, there is no impossibility.

Be Authentic!

Printed in Great Britain
by Amazon

44180839R00118